sh[OUT]:

Contemporary art and human rights
Lesbian, gay, bisexual, transgender and intersex art and culture

- Patricia Cronin
- Nan Goldin
- Felix Gonzalez-Torres
- Sunil Gupta
- David Hockney
- Holly Johnson
- Deborah Kass
- Ins A Kromminga
- Sadie Lee
- Chad McCail
- Robert Mapplethorpe
- Catherine Opie
- Grayson Perry
- Pierre et Gilles
- Jack Pierson
- Lizzie Rowe
- Diane Torr
- Del LaGrace Volcano

Published in April 2009 by Glasgow Museums Publishing.

ISBN 978 0902752 90 0

Edited by: Sean McGlashan and Fiona MacLeod
Designed and typeset by: Ashley Rawson
Printed in Scotland by Allander Print.

sh[OUT], Gallery of Modern Art, Glasgow, Scotland, 9 April–1 November 2009. *sh[OUT]* is a Culture and Sport Glasgow (Museums) project, developed in partnership with Amnesty International and supported with funding from Culture and Sport Glasgow, the Scottish Arts Council and Show Scotland.

Table of Contents

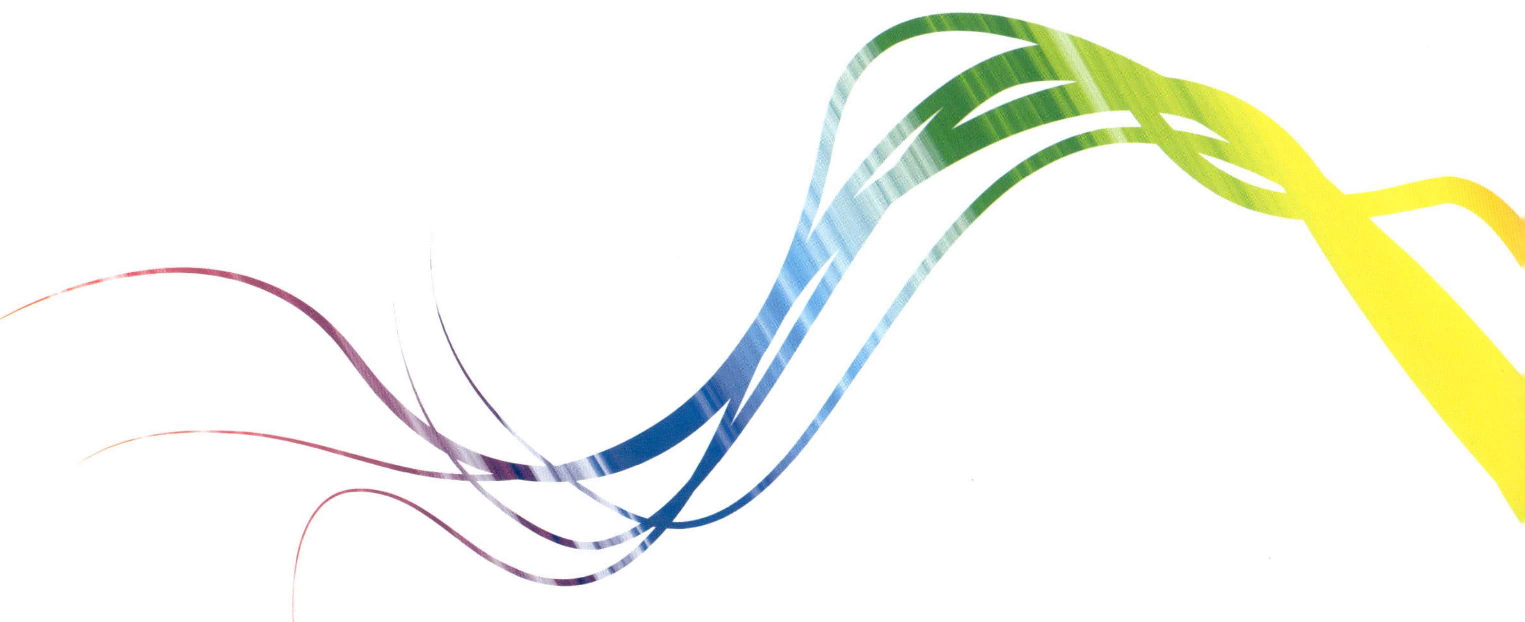

"Glasgow has **a long history of supporting human rights**"

Glasgow has a long history of supporting human rights and we are proud to have received refugees from the Spanish Civil War, children from the Kindertransports from Nazi Germany and more recently asylum seekers from many of the world's most troubled countries. The battle for the rights of local people date back at least to the Weavers' strike of 1787, and continued throughout the nineteenth and twentieth centuries. Though benefiting from slavery in the tobacco plantations of the Caribbean, Glasgow later became a centre for the anti-slavery movement, which in turn inspired the women's suffrage campaigns. We are proud to continue this tradition by raising awareness of the issues faced daily by lesbians, gay men, bisexual, transgender and intersex people, both here in the UK and abroad. Scotland has been leading the way in terms of challenging prejudice and promoting equality, being the first country in the UK to repeal Section 2A of the Local Government Act 1986, embracing civil partnerships, and having Europe's only government-funded post in transgender rights – the Scottish Transgender Alliance Project Coordinator.

Glasgow itself is a strong community and I am proud to work for a city that supports Glasgay!, Europe's largest queer multi-arts festival. Now, through the Gallery of Modern Art's leading work on social justice and human rights, we have the opportunity to profile these issues more widely through a dynamic and innovative arts programme. In a year that marks the fortieth anniversary of the Stonewall riots in New York, it is significant that we are celebrating the art and culture of LGBT people and raising awareness of their human rights in the heart of this great city.

Bailie Liz Cameron, *Chair of Culture and Sport Glasgow*

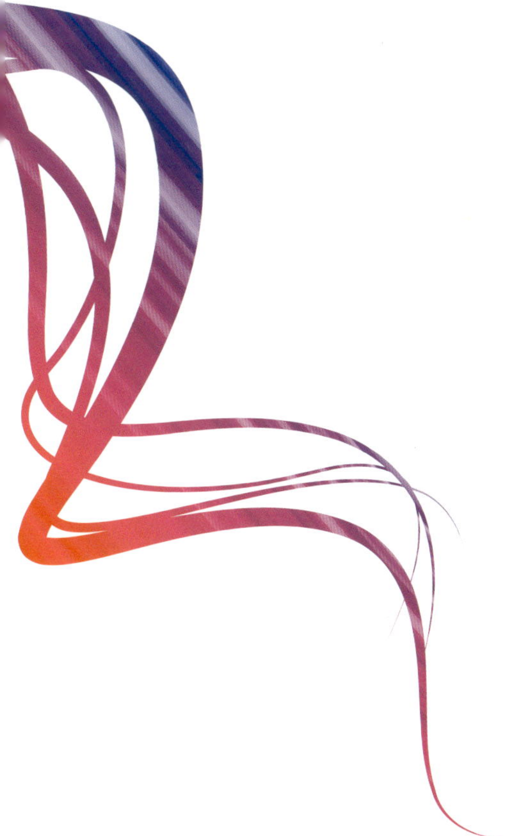

Foreword Amnesty International

"love
is a
human
right"

The links between art and human rights are strong. Artists have always valued freedom of thought and expression as a necessary condition of their creativity. It is no coincidence that artists of all disciplines have been at the forefront of movements for freedom and equality. Hundreds of writers, playwrights, musicians, and poets have been adopted by Amnesty as Prisoners of Conscience – Václav Havel, Hong Song Dam and Aung San Suu Kyi, to name but a few.

The role of art in challenging perceptions, exploring identity and reaching out to the public imagination is crucial and Amnesty International welcomes the *sh[OUT]* exhibition and applauds the ongoing commitment shown by GoMA's contemporary art and human rights social justice programme.

All over the world lesbians, gay men, bisexual, transgender and intersex people are being criminalized, tortured or ill-treated because of their sexuality. The Universal Declaration of Human Rights is clear as to 'the inherent dignity and of the equal and inalienable rights of all members of the human family'. Yet the reality is often very different for LGBT communities.

Here in the UK, 40 years since the decriminalization of homosexuality, prejudice remains and attitudes are resistant to change. The residual hostility towards LGBT people is felt by many in their day-to-day lives and has risen to the surface, for example, in the public debate around the repeal of Section 2A in 2000 and the more recent discussions around extending the definition of hate crime to include LGBT people.

Yet we know from long experience that attitudes can change. Amnesty International is pleased to support this important contribution to the continuing work that takes us beyond mere tolerance and demands full equality and respect for all.

Kate Allen, *Director of Amnesty International UK*
Contact arts@amnesty.org.uk for more information or visit www.amnesty.org.uk.

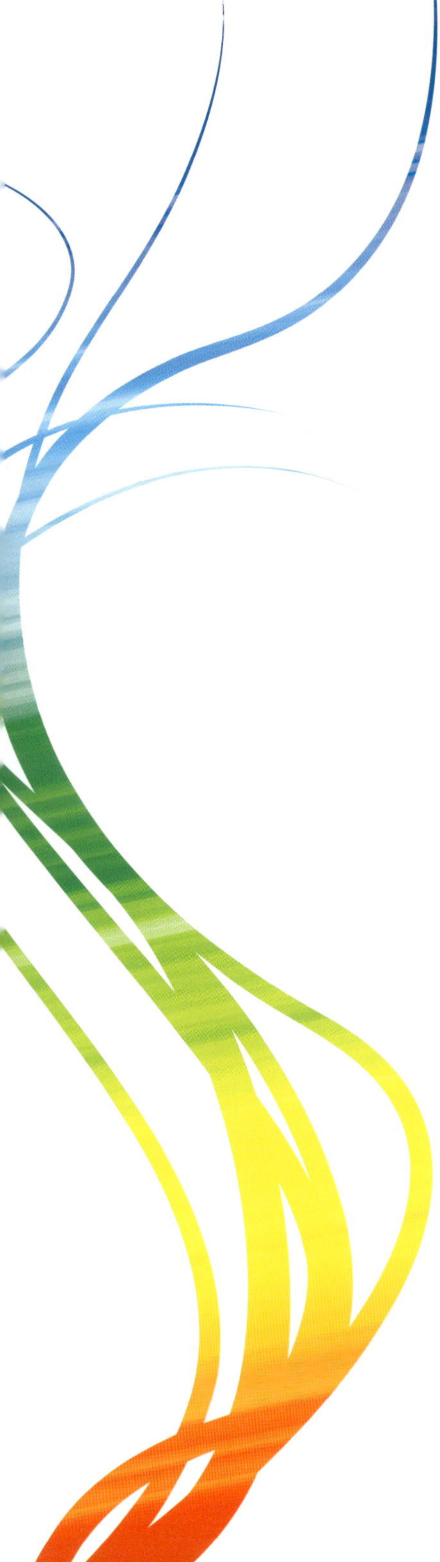

Preface Victoria Hollows

Love is a human right.

Toes entwined. A small gesture, a very powerful statement. Patricia Cronin's *Memorial To A Marriage* is a silent and enduring reminder of what we long for when all else is stripped away. In our happiest times, our darkest hours, or simply at the end of yet another busy day.

Love.
To be held by someone who loves you, to feel safe, to feel at home, eyes closed, restful, comfortable. Expressed deeply by entwining toes, an almost subconscious gesture of connection. Of all the works in this exhibition, this one will surely convey in the starkest and simplest terms this most fundamental human right.

Contemporary art and human rights is a series of programmes that forms the central, distinguishing feature of GoMA's overall aim. They began in 2001 with a commitment from Glasgow City Council to fund biennial exhibitions on human rights themes. We have addressed issues of asylum seekers and refugees, violence against women and more recently sectarianism. Each programme includes a range of exhibitions accompanied by a city-wide community engagement strategy, with the objective that both be of the highest quality and international scope.

The overwhelming success of this work, not only in raising awareness of very complex issues, but also in terms of profiling GoMA as a leading contemporary art gallery, has led to extensive recognition for our achievements. In our 2007 book *Towards an Engaged Gallery*, we discussed the previous social justice exhibitions and described the processes through which they were achieved. GoMA's work in this field is now the subject of analysis for a larger, international research project. It explores the relationship that museums and galleries have with local human rights debates, moral codes and conventions. This research, initiated by Richard Sandell from the University of Leicester, investigates leading-edge work in this field to better understand the part that cultural institutions can play in engaging visitors and society more broadly, in debates around often challenging rights-related issues.

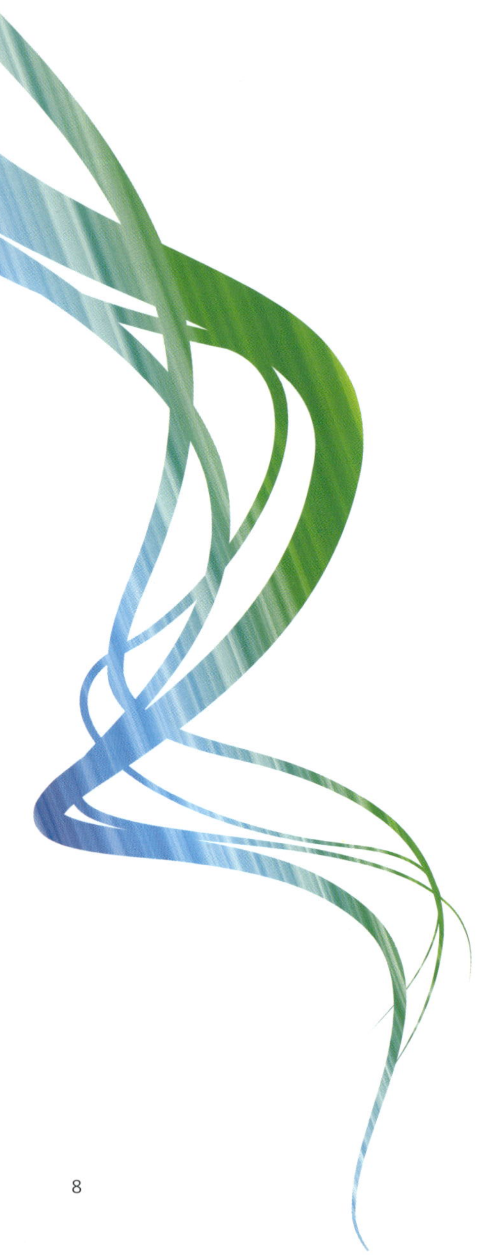

Our work at GoMA continues. *sh[OUT]: Contemporary art and human rights* is the title for the fourth social justice programme, promoting respect of lesbian, gay, bisexual, transgender and intersex (LGBT) human rights. It includes outreach projects and exhibitions, educational arts workshops, arts events, acquisitions and residencies. There is a strong international dimension to this work which is profiled particularly in the programme's central exhibition, *sh[OUT]*, whose artists are featured in this catalogue.

The entire programme has been many years in the making and central to its development have been our partners, including Amnesty International, BiScotland, the Equality Network, Gay Men's Health, the Glasgay! Festival, Glasgow LGBT Centre, LGBT Youth Scotland, LGBT History Month, OurStory Scotland, Stonewall Scotland, Trans Men Scotland and the Terrence Higgins Trust Scotland.

With these organizations we established an Advisory Board who worked with GoMA to develop aims and objectives for *sh[OUT]* in addition to providing key advice and contacts for the programme. Without them and their vital input the scope and quality of this work would not have been possible and we are indebted to them all for their generosity of time, information and creative thinking.

Our work, as with all our contemporary art and human rights programmes, is an important, public step forward in promoting acceptance and understanding. Perhaps a small step amongst the work of many others, yet the potency of contemporary art to challenge attitudes and to encourage debate is well documented through the last eight years of GoMA's work. A small step it might be, but sometimes the smallest gesture can be amongst the most powerful.

Love is a human right.

Victoria Hollows, *Museum Manager, Gallery of Modern Art*

I have been one of the two contemporary art curators working at the Gallery of Modern Art (GoMA) for over 10 years now. I have worked on many different and exciting exhibitions but this one has been more personal for me. As a gay man, putting this exhibition together has been a challenging and sometimes emotional experience. I say 'emotional' because the one thing that kept coming across to me from the many different art works was the sheer bravery of the artists. I was impressed by the pride and conviction they have when confronted with an often indifferent world.

At the beginning I could only think of a few artists but after my initial research trips to New York and London I found many artists working in this area. Limiting the scope of the exhibition was going to be a tough challenge.

"LGBT artists…"

Lesbian, gay, bisexual, transgender and intersex art and culture is a very big topic. But LGBT artists are not some new phenomenon – for instance art historians have debated the sexuality of artists such as Michelangelo and Da Vinci in recent times, and it is now generally accepted that both were homosexual. What *is* new is that in the twentieth century there was a substantial increase in the number of *out* LGBT artists, although their work does not always celebrate or address LGBT culture. The work in this exhibition *does* definitely reflect that culture, though I knew from the beginning we would not be able to cover every issue relating to LGBT people, because of the diversity of the topics-within-topics under the umbrella term 'LGBT'. As a result of this, I decided to select figurative works in traditional media that are mainly concerned with pride, confidence and the respect of differences within these groups. I have tried as much as possible to strike a balance of works by men and women that vary in theme – from the public to the private – in reflecting LGBT life.

Many of the artists come from the US and the UK; however I have also included artists originally from Canada, Cuba, France, Germany and India. In the course of my research it became apparent that there was a noticeable lack of work commenting on bisexuality.

For that reason alone there are few works in the show that speak specifically on that topic, although I am unsure as to why there should be such a gulf.
It remains an unanswered question.

Some of the artists are famous and others are less well known, but all of them have practices that reflect and investigate alternative sexualities. Not all are formally trained, although many have studied at universities and arts institutions and continue to teach the next generation of future practitioners.

It is important to realize that at the end of the day, lesbian, gay, bisexual, transgender and intersex people are not just seeking tolerance. We are looking for respect.

Sean McGlashan, *Curator, Contemporary Art*

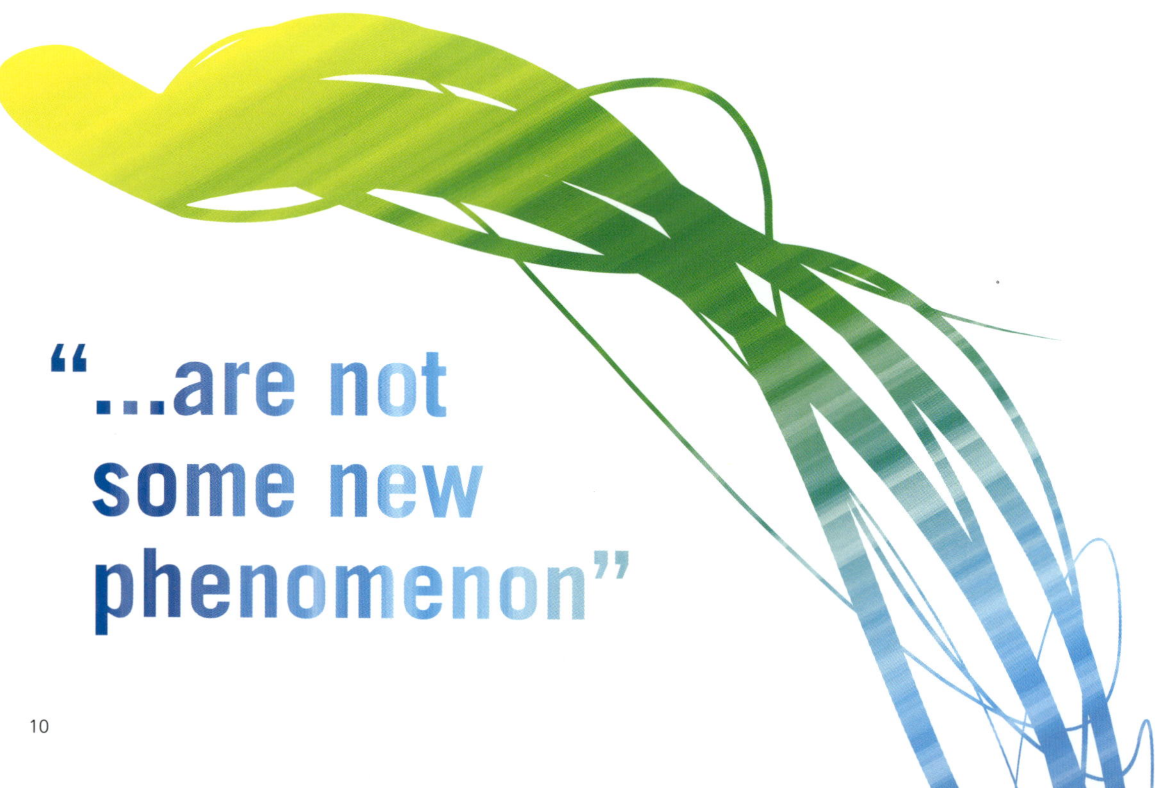

"...are not some new phenomenon"

In early discussions for the *sh[OUT]* programme, a key concern for organizations and individuals in the LGBT community was the continual regulation of sexuality and gender identity by society. Although Scotland has made progress through legislation and attitude changes, tolerance is not the same as respect. Our outreach and schools programmes are an opportunity for us to facilitate debate, to share ideas, and hopefully move towards a greater understanding of each other.

The exhibition celebrates LGBT and intersex lives, art and culture, and provides space for further exploration of attitudes. The broader *sh[OUT]* programme expands on ideas of family, community, safety, identity, body, sexuality, prejudice, tolerance and faith. Our intention is not that the programme should attempt to provide all-encompassing answers about sexuality, but rather that it should provoke discussion and debate around society's apparent need to regulate gender, sexuality and identity.

Outreach projects will involve artists Julie Ballands, Dianne Barry, Jane McInally, Anthony Schrag and David Sherry collaborating with groups such as LGBT Youth Scotland, the Scottish Transgender Alliance and the Metropolitan Community Church. They hope to develop new work together around the themes the programme raises such as health, disability, identity and faith. Work from these outreach projects is a key part of the Balcony exhibition programme at GoMA; one of the *sh[OUT]*/OurStory Scotland partnerships showcases the work of Kate Charlesworth and David Shenton in *Drawn Out & Painted Pink*.

Petra Kuppers and Neil Marcus are in residence at Tramway, the performing arts venue, promoting their new book *Cripple Poetics – A Love Story*. They explore disability and sexuality in an extremely intimate manner, challenging narrowly defined assumptions around sexuality generally. A series of performances and readings in the city will form part of Tramway's ongoing education programme.

The Glasgay! Festival is a key event in Glasgow's calendar, and we have developed elements of the *sh[OUT]* programme, such as performance, film and discussions, with the organizers. Dani Marti's residency will be based at Glasgay!

> "The reward for conformity is that everyone likes you..."

He intends to collaborate with organizations already working with LGBT groups and individuals, such as Strathclyde Police, Gay Men's Heath, LGBT Youth Scotland and the Open Road Project. Outcomes from this work will be seen at both the Q! Gallery and in GoMA.

A further two residencies are planned, with artists spending three months at GoMA followed by three months at Trongate 103 (a space which houses exhibition spaces and artists' production facilities). This is the first time we, in conjunction with Culture and Sport Glasgow's Arts Development Team, have been able to offer a mentoring opportunity for a disabled or deaf artist as part of the social justice programmes.

sh[OUT]-related cabaret, film and music events will also feature in Show Scotland 2009, an annual creative cultural events weekend celebrating Scotland's museums and galleries. There will be workshops for adults and young people, as well as a programme of talks by artists and curators.

The wider *sh[OUT]* programme involves visits by community groups to GoMA, with practical workshops and exhibition visits inviting further discussion and exploration of the topic. The Schools Programme reflects on existing external good practice – such as respect*me* and LGBT Youth Scotland's Toolkit for Teachers (see References) – all recently developed for schools. Secondary schools can explore the exhibitions and related issues of LGBT and intersex human rights. Key to this will be a freelance artist who will develop and deliver the programme with our own staff, alongside ongoing consultation with external organizations.

Community workshops sit alongside the Schools Programme, and in the Read, Relax, Respond Space in Gallery 4 we provide further information on the exhibition and its related topics. Lastly, artists Janie Nicoll and Alex Hetherington are exploring how we can document the strands that make up *sh[OUT]: Contemporary art and human rights*, making this visible during the programme – and as a legacy of the work.

Katie Bruce, *Social Inclusion Coordinator* and Frances McCourt, *Learning & Access Curator*

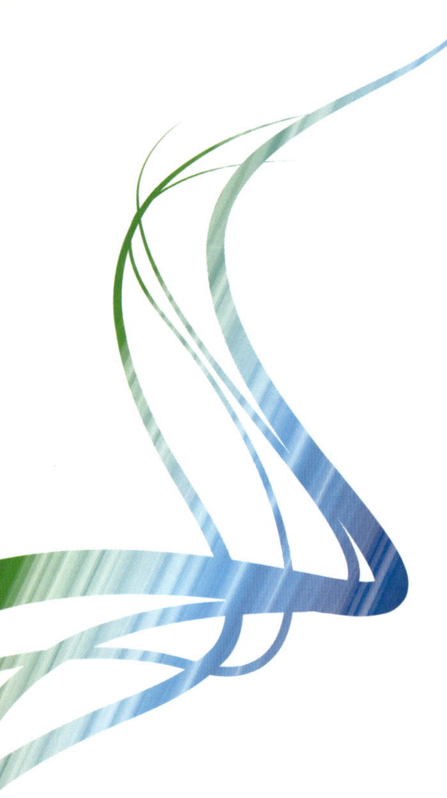

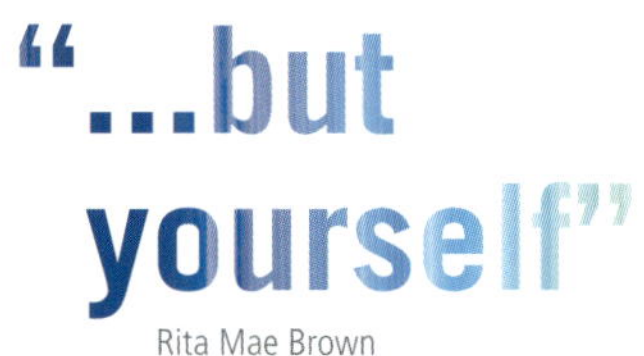

Rita Mae Brown

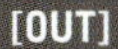

sh[OUT]: Artists

Patricia Cronin

Patricia Cronin's paintings, sculptures and installations have been exhibited extensively in the US and Europe, including at the American Academy in Rome and and the COBRA Museum, Amsterdam. Born in 1963, in Beverly, Massachusetts, Cronin trained at Brooklyn College in New York, Rhode Island College, Skowhegan School of Painting and Sculpture and at Yale University Summer School.

Her work has been critically acclaimed in numerous publications including the *The New York Times* and *Artforum*. Cronin is the recipient of many awards and grants, including the Rome Prize at the American Academy in Rome and a Civitella Ranieri Foundation Fellowship in Umbria, Italy. 'A Perfect Affection', a 30-minute documentary on Cronin's art practice, was produced in 2004 for The Gallery Channel on HD TV. It was subsequently a finalist for a Telly Award.

She is currently an Associate Professor of Art at Brooklyn College of The City University of New York.

www.patriciacronin.net

'I manipulate and reinvigorate traditional, art historical forms and inject them with my specific contemporary content. Everything from oil portraits, erotic watercolours, equestrian sculptures, neo-classical funerary monuments to public art and installation art utilizing time honoured artists' materials – paint, clay, plaster, bronze and marble – to address contemporary issues of sexuality, gender and class. I rely on the seduction of the familiar and very gently disrupt the viewer's expectations.

Deborah (my partner, the artist Deborah Kass) and I have all the legal documents one can have to try to simulate the legal protections of marriage, but they are wills, health care proxies and power-of-attorney documents. They are so depressing because they are all about if one of us gets incapacitated or dies. I wanted something official that celebrated our life together and if all I will be officially allowed is death, I decided to make the most elegant and dignified statement I could about the end of our life together.

In 2002 I created *Memorial To A Marriage*, an over life-size three ton Carrara marble mortuary sculpture, which is a double portrait of Deborah and me. It is permanently installed on our actual burial plot in the Woodlawn Cemetery, in New York. Woodlawn was designed as America's equivalent to the Père Lachaise Cemetery in Paris and is one of the pre-eminent examples of the Garden or Rural Cemetery Movement. *Memorial To A Marriage* is public art in that the Woodlawn Cemetery is open to the public free of charge everyday and is on view through eternity. The statue addresses issues of lesbian invisibility, gay marriage, love and loss, power and status. In this sculpture I chose a nationalist form – nineteenth-century American neo-classical sculpture – to address what I consider a federal failure. In death I make official my "marriage" which is still not legal while we are alive.'

Memorial To A Marriage
2004
Bronze
134.6cm x 67.3cm x 43.1cm
© Patricia Cronin

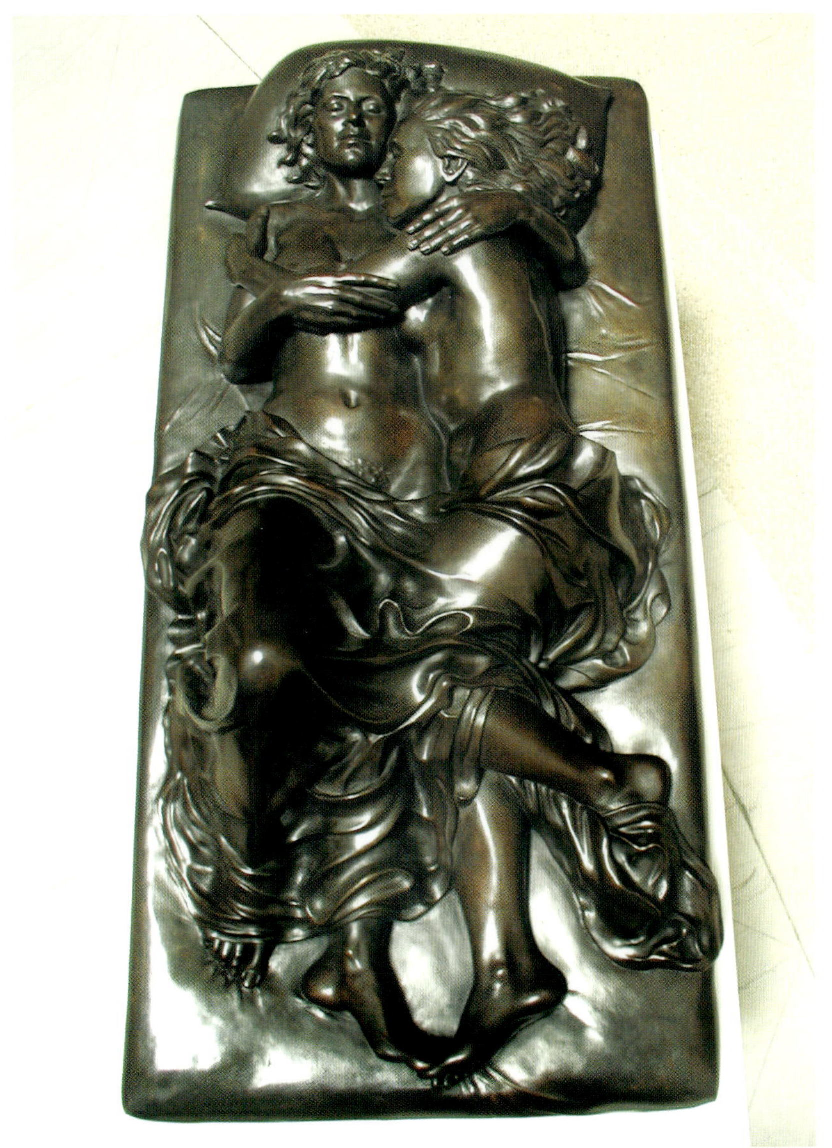

Nan Goldin

Celebrated photographer Nan Goldin is noted for documenting New York City's vibrant, post-Stonewall subculture of the late 1970s and early 1980s, work that is symptomatic of her life-long fascination with the fine line dividing the genders.

Born in Washington DC in 1953, Nan left home at the age of 15, moving in with foster families, and learning photography at school. Her first solo show, in 1973, was based on Goldin's photographic sojourns among the city's gay and transsexual communities. In the late 1970s she graduated from the School of the Museum of Fine Arts, Boston and moved to New York City.

Goldin's work – in her 'snapshot' style – subsequently focused on her friends in New York, documenting their day-to-day lives. It was here that she developed her most famous work, *The Ballad of Sexual Dependency*, a body of photographs that details scenes of abusive relationships and hard drug use. Winner of the 2007 Hasselblad Award, Goldin lives in New York and Paris.

This composite image shows Greer Lankton, long-term friend, flatmate and muse of Nan Goldin. It spans moments in Lankton's life across several decades, capturing her in deeply personal, unguarded scenes. One view appears to show Lankton getting married, whilst in another she lies in the bath, studiously avoiding meeting the camera's gaze.

Photography can freeze time and enhance our memories, which is Goldin's main concern in her work. The eccentricity of her close circle of friends makes her snapshot style of working very engaging. We are allowed into a world that is familiar to some, and utterly alien to others.

Lankton was herself both a successful artist and a transsexual. She died from anorexia in 1996. Her installations often featured dolls, images of which are included in Goldin's photographic montage. The dolls went through various transformations, some gaining and losing weight, others appearing with stitches in the bodies to suggest surgical procedures. They reflected Lankton's position on the gender divide and allowed her to comment on society's pressure upon women to fit an impossible ideal of appearance.

Greer Lankton, 21 April 1958 – 18 November 1996
1979–1995/1998
15 mounted cibachrome prints
155cm x 183cm
© Nan Goldin, Courtesy Matthew Marks Gallery, New York

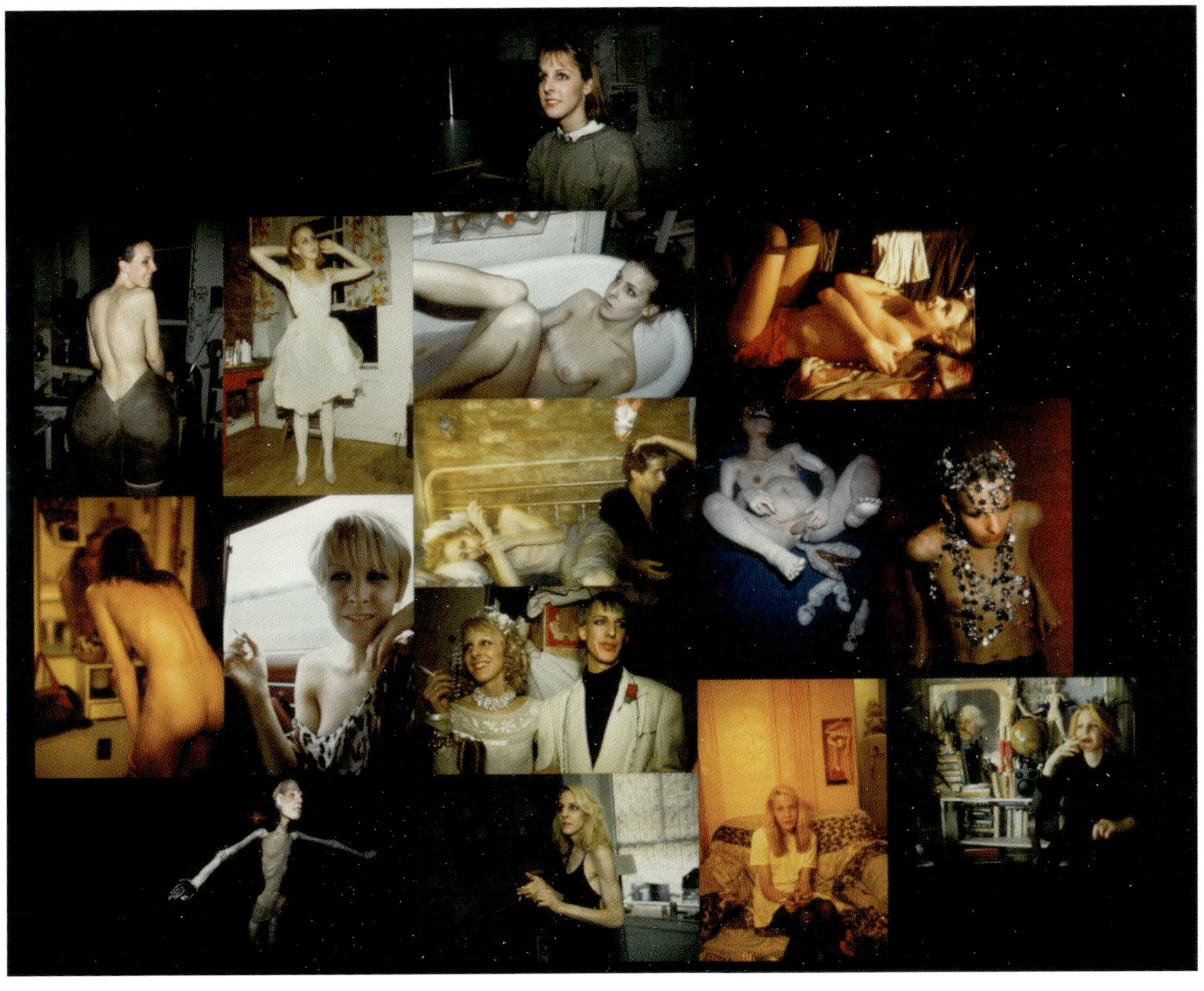

Felix Gonzalez-Torres

Felix Gonzalez-Torres was a conceptual artist, taking as his inspiration the theme of love and lovers, exploring aspects of his own relationships and the subsequent death of his partner, Ross, to illustrate the feeling of loss. He is recognized for his minimal, peaceful installations which invite the viewer in some cases to literally take a piece of the art away, a bit at a time, as in his confectionery installations.

Born in Guaimaro, Cuba in 1957, he grew up in Puerto Rico, later moving to Spain and the US. He studied at the Pratt Institute in Brooklyn and received a Master of Fine Arts degree from the International Center of Photography and New York University in 1987.

He has been the subject of several retrospectives, notably at the Guggenheim Museum in New York and at the Serpentine Gallery in London. In 2002 the Felix Gonzalez-Torres Foundation was created to safeguard his work for future generations, and in 2007 he posthumously represented the US at the Venice Biennale. He died in 1996.

The significance of these clocks lies partly in the fact that they are every day, generic objects found in all spheres of life, from the public realm of the office through to the private world of the home. They disappear into the background. They are standard, inexpensive clocks, found coast-to-coast throughout North America and around the world.

For Gonzalez-Torres they provided the perfect vehicle for commenting on his relationship with his dying long-term partner Ross, as they are identical, creating a metaphor for 'same sex love in perfect unison'. They may start ticking at the same time but slowly and surely they eventually begin to fall out of unison.

"Untitled" (Perfect Lovers), 1987–1990
wall clocks
35.6cm x 71.2cm x 7cm overall
2 parts: 35.6cm diameter each
edition of 3, 1 A.P.
Photo: Peter Muscato
From the Collection of Alice and Marvin Kosmin
© The Felix Gonzalez-Torres Foundation, Courtesy Andrea Rosen Gallery, New York

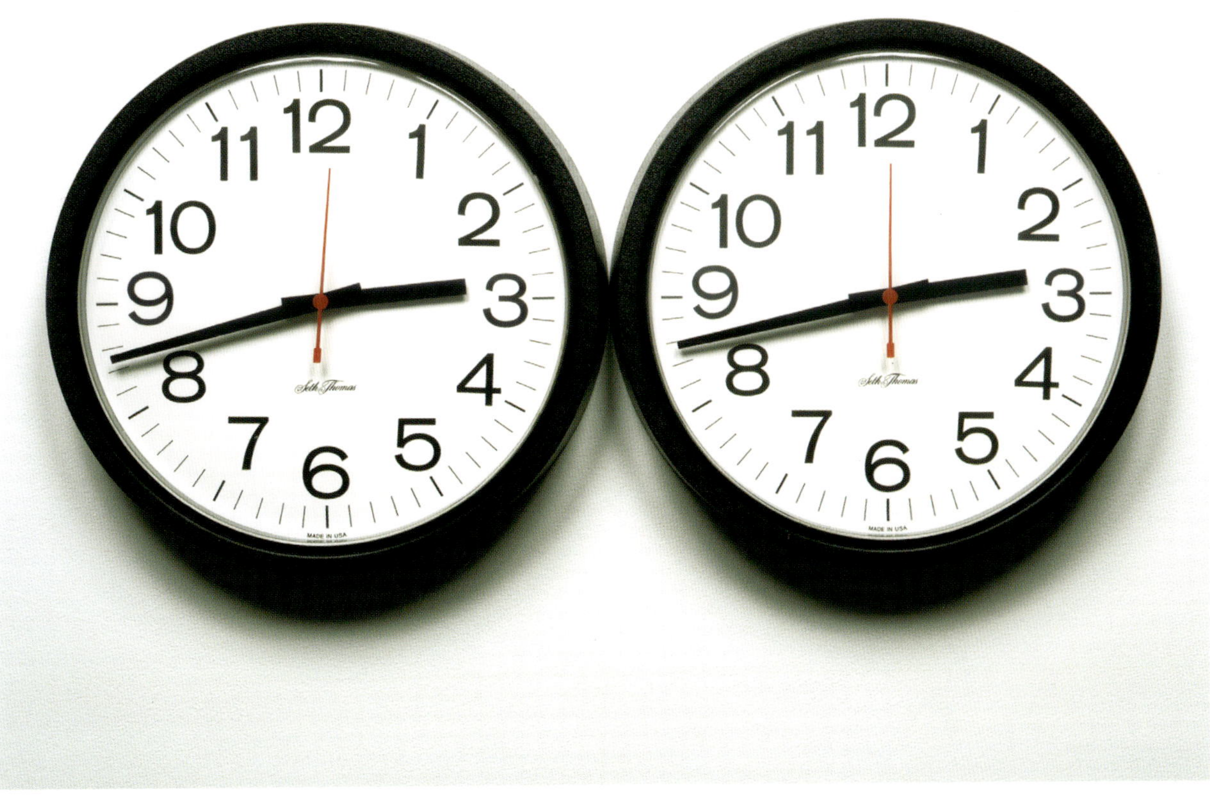

Born in New Delhi in 1953, and growing up watching Bollywood films in all their glorious colour, Sunil Gupta moved to Montreal with his family in the late1960s, where his interest in photography began to develop. Later he studied photography at the New School for Social Research then moved to London to continue his studies at the Royal College of Art, where he gained an MA in 1983. He was involved in the founding of Autograph ABP (Association of Black Photographers), and also set up the Organisation for Visual Arts (OVA).

Gupta's series *Exiles* and *Mr Malhotra's Party* are included in the 2009 exhibition *India Moderna*, at IVAM, Valencia, Spain. His book *Wish You Were Here: Memories of a Gay Life* was published in October 2008. He is completing a documentary film, 'Dead in the Water' (TBC) about access to treatment for HIV patients in the Indian public health sector for the Human Rights Law Network, and is also co-editor of *Camerawork Delhi*. Gupta currently works as a photographer, writer and curator in London and Delhi.

www.sunilgupta.net

'In the 1980s a vexing question surfaced: why wasn't I living in India? As a gay man living in the West I was in danger of losing my Indian identity. There didn't seem to be too many other gay Indians around, not on the gay scene, nor amongst activists and certainly not on the art history circuit. Surely I couldn't be the first? I knew from having lived in India as a child and having returned there that there was homosexual activity. It just seemed to lack cultural expression. In my comings and goings to make pictures in India I had explored this informally, and later with the serious purpose of helping contribute to a cultural history.

Exploring the Indian gay scene as an adult I found an intimidating wall of silence. Those (gays) I met in India lived a marginalized existence, giving in to communal pressures to maintain a "normal" front. A few at the top and the bottom of the social and political ladder were privileged enough to side step these pressures. Very few who identified with the secret "dirty habit", even those who labelled themselves gay, felt able to come out from this self-imposed internal exile. News of gains made by gay activists in the West to foster a positive gay identity and culture filtered in, but their tactics could not be exactly duplicated in India. On the other hand, HIV/AIDS arrived to reinforce all the worst stereotypes, the most common of which was that homosexuality is some terrible Western disease.'

India Gate
1987
C-type print
48.2cm x 48.2cm
© Sunil Gupta

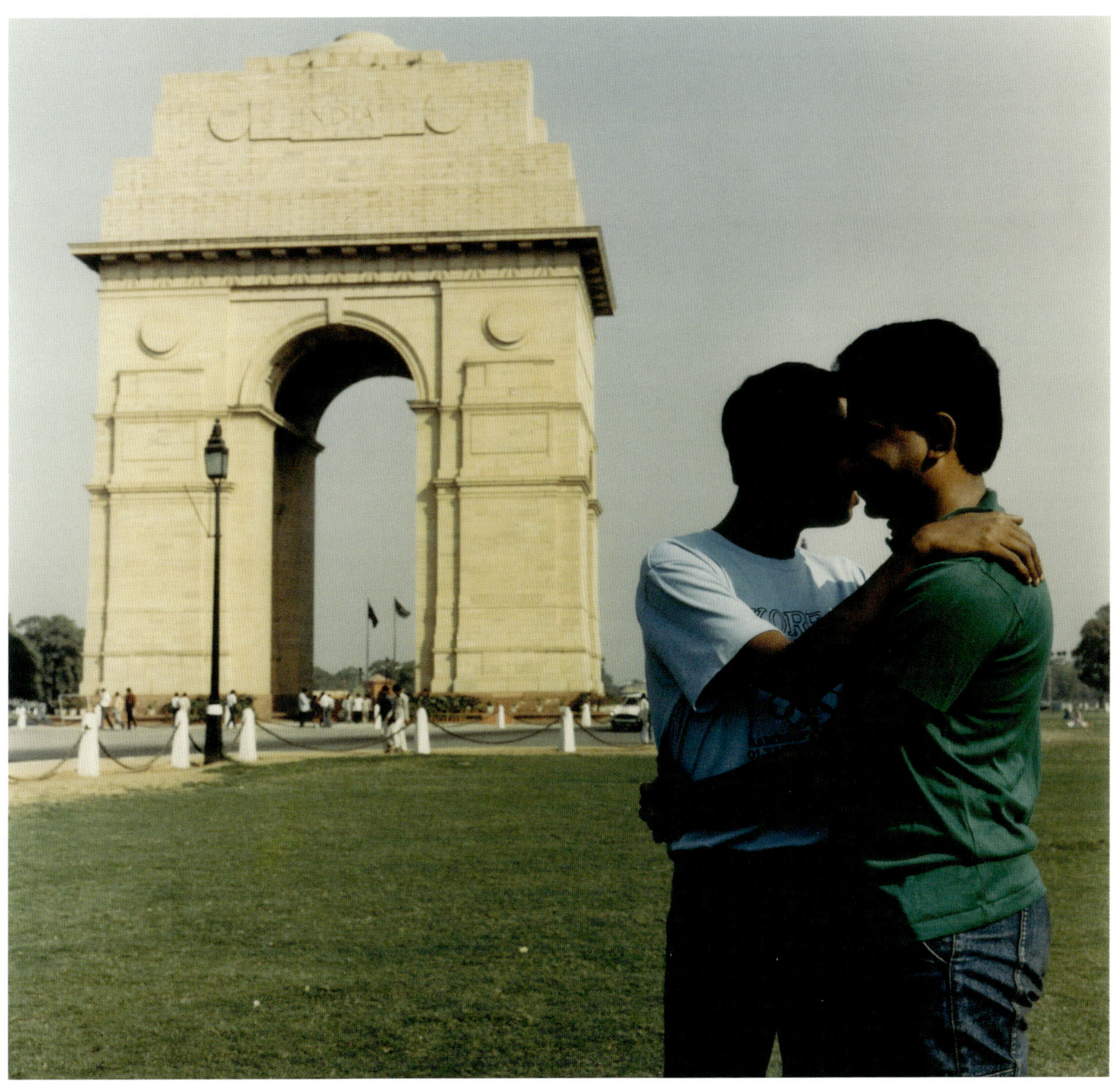

'Even if you have a lover you should get married and have children. Who would look after you in old age.'

David **Hockney**

David Hockney is one of the UK's foremost artists. He was born in Yorkshire in 1937 and studied at Bradford College of Art and at the Royal College of Art in London. In the early 1960s he featured in the explosive exhibition *Young Contemporaries*, from which arose the British Pop Art movement. Unlike many young men of that era, Hockney chose not to hide his sexuality and occasionally refers to it in his art, as in *We Two Boys Together Clinging*, making it an iconic painting for many gay men.

Hockney's work spans various mediums, including photocollage and print making. In 1998 he produced 60 canvases which combined to create an enormous collage picture titled *A Bigger Grand Canyon*, a work which is in the permanent collection of the National Gallery of Australia. Hockney is the recipient of many awards and accolades, including the Royal College of Art's Gold Medal and the Royal Photographic Society's Special Anniversary Medal. He lives and works in Yorkshire.

www.hockneypictures.com

One of his earliest famous works – part of a series of frankly homosexual works created by Hockney in the 1960s – this painting has the unique position of being the oldest work in the exhibition at GoMA. With some influences inspired by early British and American abstract artists, Hockney's main source of motivation for this painting stems from a poem of the same title by American writer Walt Whitman. The poem represents Whitman's ideal of a passionate male relationship.

Adorned in graffiti-like phrases, the imagery seems to show a yearning to return to a child's innocence of desire. The lines of text on the right-hand side of the painting – below the heart – are from the fourth and fifth lines of the poem:

'Power enjoying, elbows stretching, fingers clutching,
Arm'd and fearless, eating, drinking, sleeping, loving.'

The numbers in the painting are code, for instance '4.8' on the left-hand figure represents Hockney himself – D is the fourth letter of the alphabet, H the eighth. Hockney used this code to camouflage the identities of his close circle of friends.

We Two Boys Together Clinging
1961
Oil on board
121.9cm x 152.4cm
© David Hockney, Courtesy Arts Council Collection, Southbank Centre London

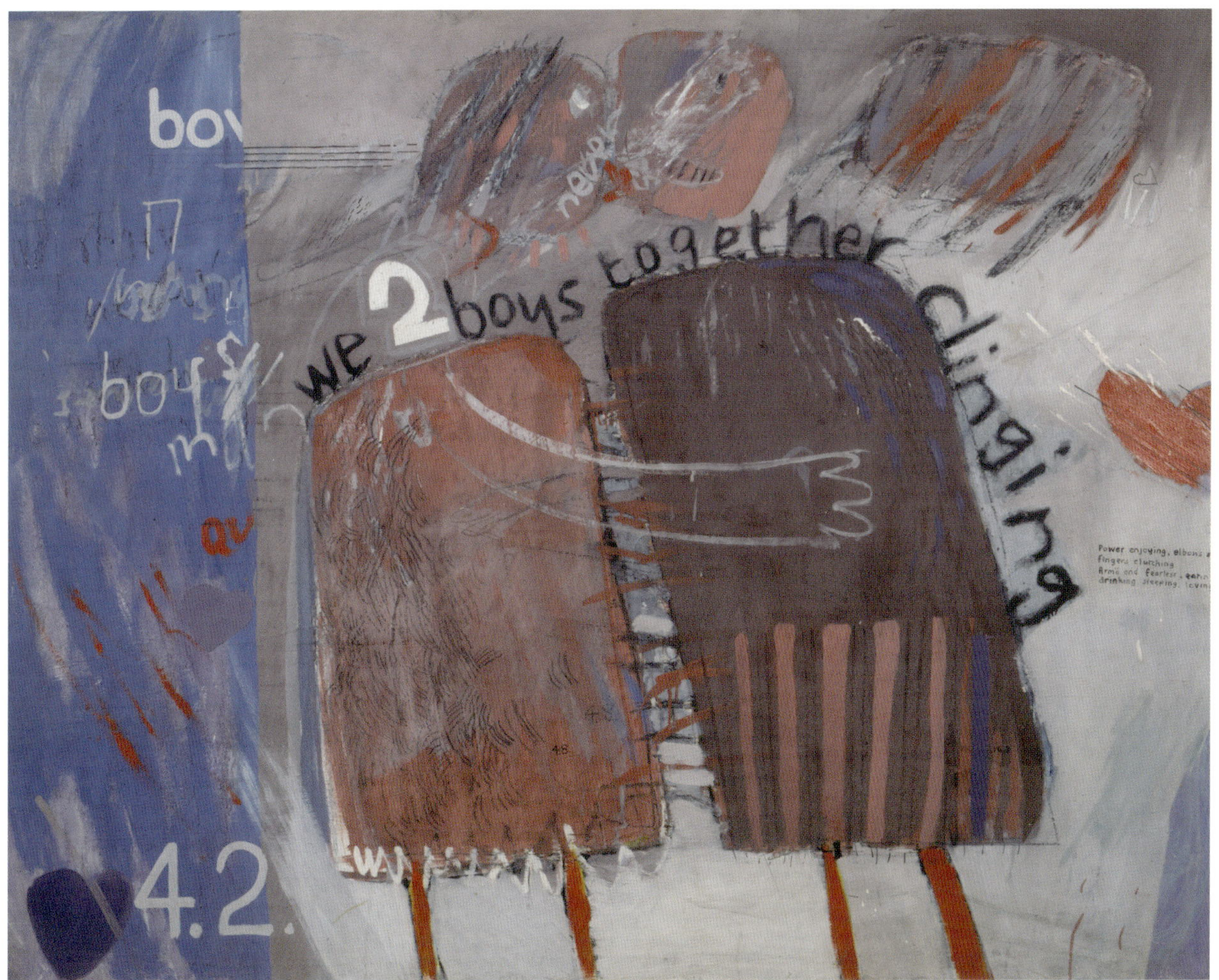
boy
boys
we 2 boys together clinging
4.2.

Holly Johnson

Holly Johnson was born near Penny Lane in Liverpool, the street made famous by the Beatles' song of the same name, in 1960. Having left Liverpool Collegiate Grammar School for Boys as soon as legally possible, he started to make silkscreen prints and art T-shirts influenced by Pop Art, Andy Warhol and David Bowie. It was not until the early 1980s that Johnson formed the band Frankie Goes to Hollywood, going on to have global success with the smash hit 'Relax'. This led him to give up a place at art college to pursue music.

Throughout this period Johnson continued to draw and paint. However, in November 1991 he discovered that he was HIV positive. The subsequent desire to write his autobiography and the process of coming to terms with his HIV status began to dominate this period of his life, although he continued to create art. Johnson has exhibited works at venues such as Tate Liverpool, the Royal Academy of Arts, the Royal College of Art and Salford Museum and Art Gallery.

www.hollyjohnson.com

'Even in contemporary art images of love and affection – platonic or sexual – expressed between individuals of the same sex are rarely seen. It was with great surprise when I turned over the pages of *The Sunday Times* on 1 January 2006 and read the headline "Mwah … is this the first gay kiss?" Next to this were placed the fragments of an Egyptian wall painting. It showed a unique depiction of two men embracing, their noses touching – the most intimate gesture allowed in the visual language of the old kingdom tombs. The article went on to describe the speculation surrounding what has become known as "The Tomb of the Hairdressers" and its potential as a honeymoon destination for those who have entered into a civil partnership.

The tomb, found in 1964 beneath the Pyramid of Unas at Saqqara, has also been described as "The Tomb of Two Brothers". Dating from the mid-Fifth Dynasty, additional images of a partially painted over wife and sons have been put forward as evidence that the figures of the two men do not portray a homosexual relationship. However, even today it is not uncommon for LGBT men and women to marry and have children – only to later come out with what they feel is their true sexual orientation. This is especially understandable in a culture where homosexuality is viewed as perverted and contrary to Islamic Sharia Law. Since 2007, 17 Egyptian men have been jailed under the guise of HIV prevention and men continue to be imprisoned and sentenced to hard labour for convictions related to homosexuality.

Personally, all of these thoughts about the modern abuses of gay men had to be put aside. Ideas of sex and sexuality faded into insignificance as I tried to piece together the fragments and imagine the colour and lamplight in which they were eternally sealed. I became fascinated by the simple beauty of an expression of love between the two people named Niankhkhnum and Khnumhotep, the overseers of the manicurists in the palace of King Niuserre. Their names translate as *Khnum* – "has life", and *Khnum* – "is satisfied" (or at peace).'

The Embrace of Niankhkhnum and Khnumhotep
2008
Oil on canvas
116cm x 89cm
© Holly Johnson

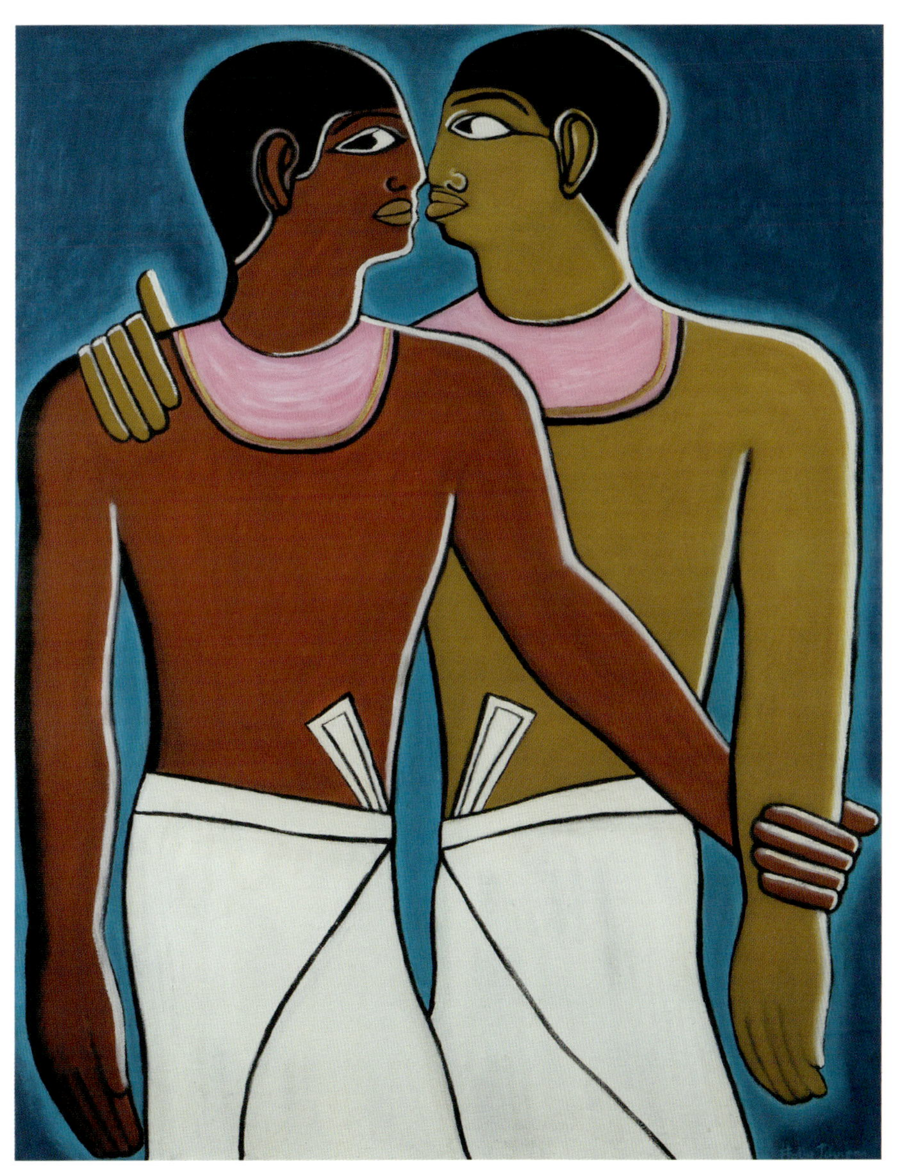

Deborah **Kass**

Deborah Kass received her Bachelor of Fine Arts degree in Painting at Carnegie-Mellon University in Pittsburgh, studied at the Whitney Museum Independent Study Program in New York and with the Art Students' League of New York. Her work is in the collections of the Museum of Modern Art, the Whitney Museum of Art, the Solomon R Guggenheim Museum and The Jewish Museum, all in New York, as well as numerous other public and private collections. Her work has been written about extensively in *The New York Times*, art press, and academic books.

A survey show, *Deborah Kass, The Warhol Project* travelled across the US from 1999–2001. Her work has been shown at the Venice Biennale, the Istanbul Biennale, and the Museum Ludwig, Cologne. She is a Senior Critic in the Yale University Master of Fine Arts Painting Program. Her work is represented by Vincent Fremont and the Paul Kasmin Gallery. Kass lives and works in Brooklyn.

www.deborahkass.com

Deborah Kass is an American artist whose paintings examine the intersection of art history, popular culture and the self. In *The Warhol Project* (1992–2000) she raided Andy Warhol's oeuvre to reinvent it in her own image, delivering both a critique and homage to Warhol and the generally accepted narrative of post-war American art history. Her love of and exclusion from that history continues to inform her work. When making her painting *Orange Deb*, Kass used the same pre-digital photo silkscreen techniques that Andy Warhol used in his well known portraits of celebrities such as Elizabeth Taylor.

Orange Deb
2000
Silkscreen on canvas
101.6cm x 101.6cm
© Courtesy of the artist and Paul Kasmin Gallery

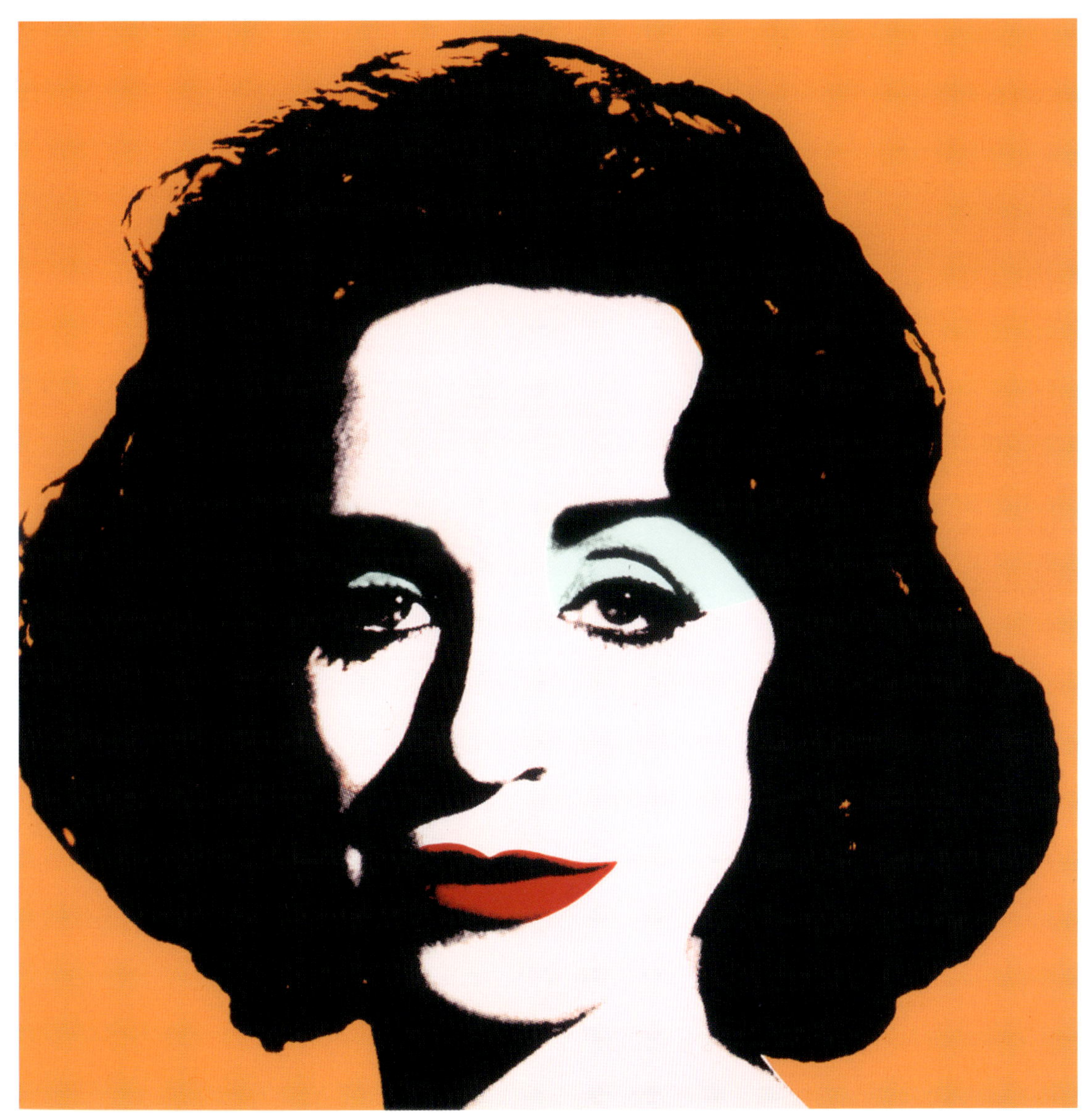

Ins A Kromminga

Ins A Kromminga was born in the small German city of Emden in 1970. After attending art classes at the local Kunsthalle as a teenager, he_she studied at the Hochschule für Künste in Bremen and later at Tulane University in New Orleans, where he_she gained a Master of Fine Arts degree.

He_She has exhibited in the US and in Europe and was included in the recent COBRA Museum exhibition *Just Different* in Amsterdam. Lately he_she has begun developing 3D designs and animation works addressing intersex issues. Kromminga lives and works in Berlin.

www.abject.de

'The topics in my work stem from my personal experiences as an intersex person. Both the creative and political inform my practice. As an activist in liberation networks such as the Berlin-based non-government organization TransInterQueer and Organization Intersex International (OII), I am part of a movement to introduce the concept of human rights for intersex people.

I am interested in the dialogues around queer politics, sex/gender, identity and the marginalization of groups of people through classification. It is a basic human right that everyone should have the freedom to make their own choices in relation to their body – a right that is not always given to intersex people.

I would like to see a shift in society's attitude towards acceptance of our differences, away from the prevailing idea that we must conform to the binary Western model of male/female. Acceptance should not have to come at the cost of our physical and mental integrity.

The mythology of hermaphrodites informs the way that society continuously fails to see intersex people. We are seen as either god-like creatures, for example as in Ovid's *Metamorphoses*, or monstrous beings, referred to as having a disorder. Both viewpoints allow society to avoid examining its own values of what constitutes "normal". *Herm Pride* represents for me a utopian ideal of a cultural shift in society away from this notion of "norms".'

Herm Pride
2009
Installation, mixed media
© Ins A Kromminga
Commissioned by Glasgow Museums, 2009

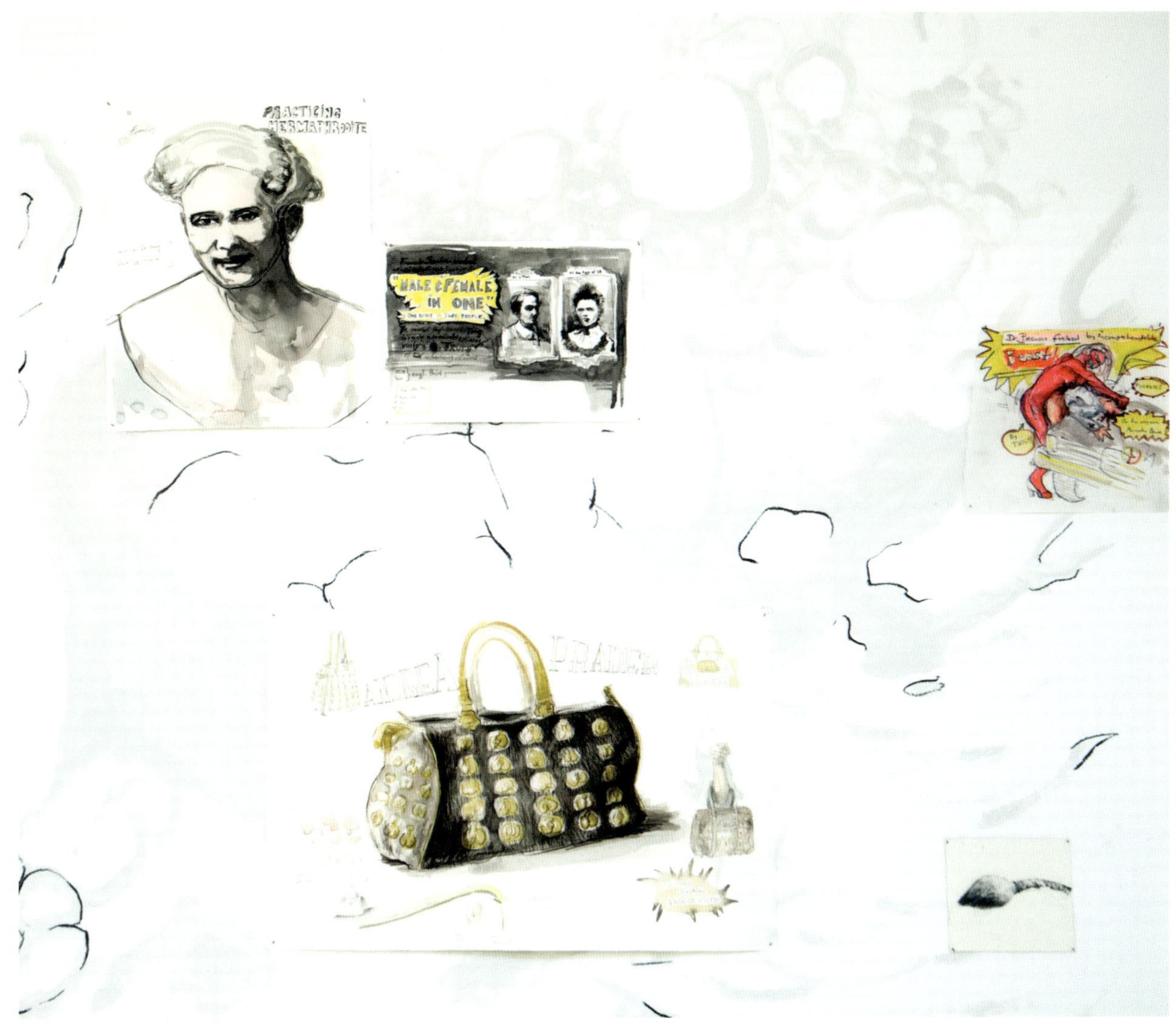
PRACTICING
HERMAPHRODITE
"MALE & FEMALE
IN ONE"
ANDREA PRADA

Sadie Lee

Sadie Lee was born in 1967. She grew up in Yorkshire and moved with her family to Surrey when she was 14. She briefly attended a foundation course in Fine Art but left without completing it to pursue an ill-thought-out modelling career. She began painting in earnest in 1992 and, despite the negative implications of the 'self-taught' tag, her first oil painting was selected for the prestigious BP Awards at the National Portrait Gallery. The painting *Erect* was used to promote the BP Awards, made into posters and displayed at every underground station across central London. To date, Lee has been selected for the BP Awards seven times, won the BP Travel Award in 1996 and was commended in 1998. Other shows include group exhibitions at the Institute of Contemporary Art, and the Museum of London. Solo shows have been held at Manchester Art Gallery and the Museum of Modern Art, Slovenia. She lives and works in London.

www.sadielee.com

'I paint real women whose appearance or behaviour may be considered inappropriate, unladylike, or otherwise render them unlikely subjects to be represented in oils.

Although very much inspired by traditional paintings of women, I am aware that they can often be represented as idealized, passive objects to be gazed at unchallenged. I am interested in my sitter's expression of her own sexuality and her awareness that she is being observed. By considering eye contact and body language, the sitter can appear more empowered, which can be an unsettling experience for the viewer.

I first began making paintings of older models in 1997 in my solo show *A Dying Art: Ladies of Burlesque* which was shown at the National Portrait Gallery in London before touring the UK for a year. This was a series of paintings of former striptease and burlesque dancers from the 1940s to the 1970s – now elderly, retired and posing in revealing costumes from their performance heydays.

And then He was a She premiered at Salford Museum and Art Gallery in 2007 and toured to The Drill Hall, London, and the Novas Contemporary Urban Centre, Liverpool. The show is a collection of paintings of Holly Woodlawn – often described as "the world's most famous drag queen". Holly Woodlawn is renowned for her stand-out performance in the Warhol film *Trash*, released to rapturous acclaim in 1970. But she is perhaps best known as the introductory character in Lou Reed's seminal song "Walk on the Wild Side". Although she is celebrated as a glamorous Warhol superstar, I painted Holly casually dressed and without make-up. Now in her sixties, this is the first time in her professional career that Holly has agreed to be presented publicly out of drag.

My paintings are increasingly about the representation of the ageing body, sexuality and the ambiguity of gender.'

Holly Woodlawn Dressing II
2007
Oil on canvas
122cm x 91cm
© Sadie Lee

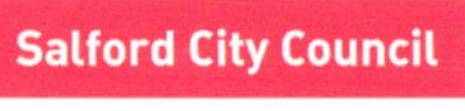
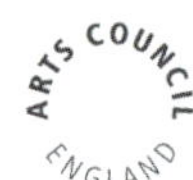
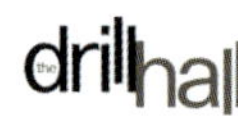

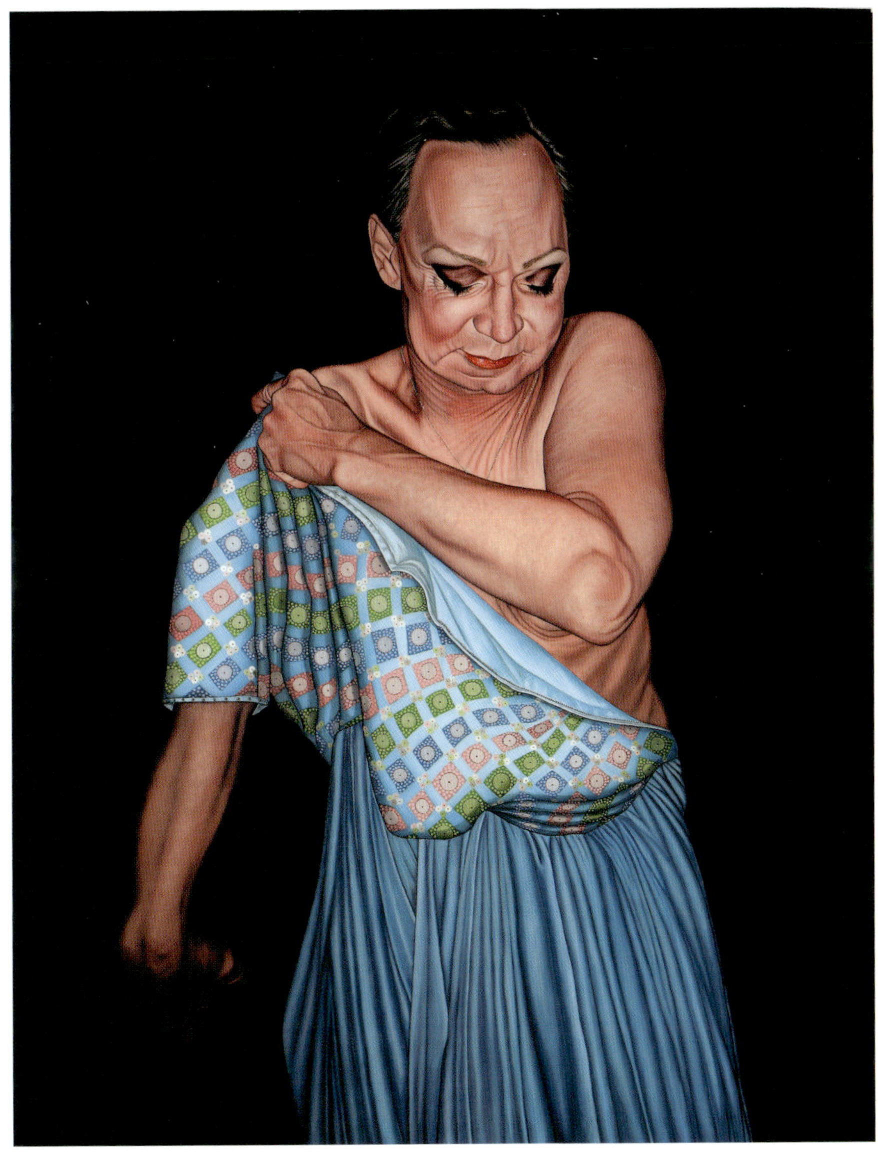

Chad **McCail**

Chad McCail was born in 1961 in Manchester and grew up in Edinburgh. He lives and works in Thankerton, South Lanarkshire. Having first read English at the University of Kent, he later graduated in Fine Art from Goldsmiths College, London, in 1989.

His work explores the links between sexual repression, violence and unquestioning obedience. Idealistic, brightly coloured paintings are accompanied by slogan-like captions and executed in a learn-to-read font. They simultaneously question both the authoritarian nature of propaganda and the objectivity of the child's textbook. His digital works are reminiscent of educational graphics, drawing on sources as varied as Egyptian hieroglyphs and vintage science fiction. He has published a graphic novel, *Active Genital* (2002), and an online sim-society game based on McCail's drawings, 'spring_alpha', has been devised by Simon Yuill. He recently completed a 40-metre-long series of panels on the history of compulsory education for exterior display in Edinburgh.

www.chadmccail.co.uk

'In Octavia Butler's novel, *Dawn* (1987), there is a scene where a man and a woman are reconciled with the alien when they make love to it simultaneously.

Because sexuality is the most intimate and delicate relationship we have with one another, because it involves us urgently, because it is bound up with taboo and fraught with anxiety and abuse, because it now has to contain almost all our everyday, tangible experience of the organic and the visceral, because it is so frequently and ubiquitously mal-imagined and connected in some way with unconscious expressions of power and violence – for all these reasons it is a compelling subject.

Spring Tree is a plant which has developed flowers which simulate human genitals. In a process somewhat akin to that developed by the bee orchid, the action of intercourse with the tree's flowers causes pollen to be transported to the stigma, bringing about the self-fertilization of the flower.

Spring Tree grew out of an earlier work, *Dream Genital* (2007), a comic story where an adolescent girl and boy acquire a mature, active sexuality in an encounter with a magical tree of genitals.

In this work I wanted to make sexuality appear exuberant, strange and unfamiliar, something intelligent and aware that uses us for its own ends.'

Spring Tree (not pictured)
2009
Papier mâché
© Chad McCail
Commissioned by Glasgow Museums,
2009

Dream Genital (pictured)
2007
Page 3 (of 5) Lamda print
© Chad McCail

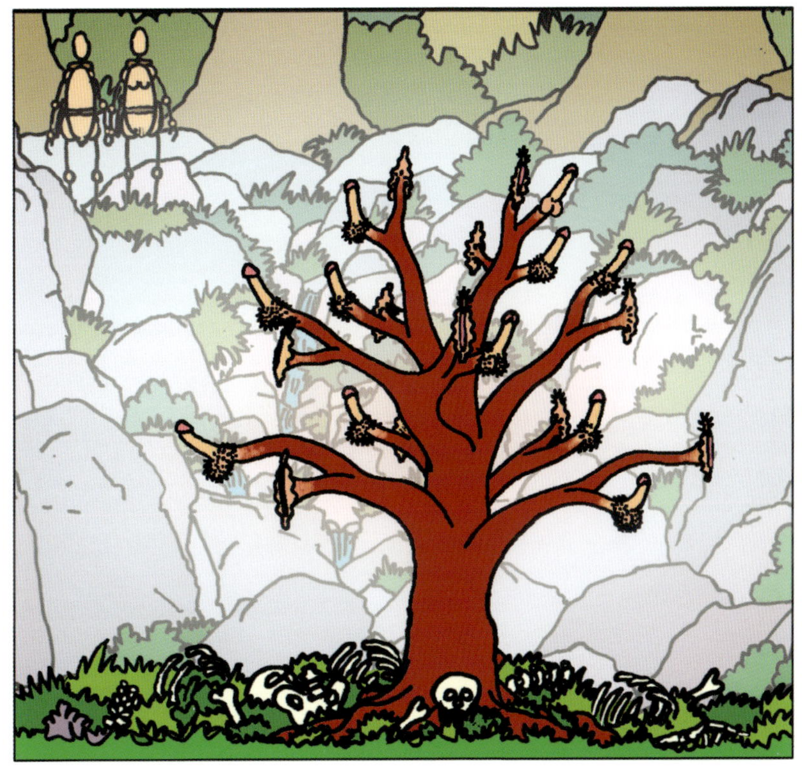

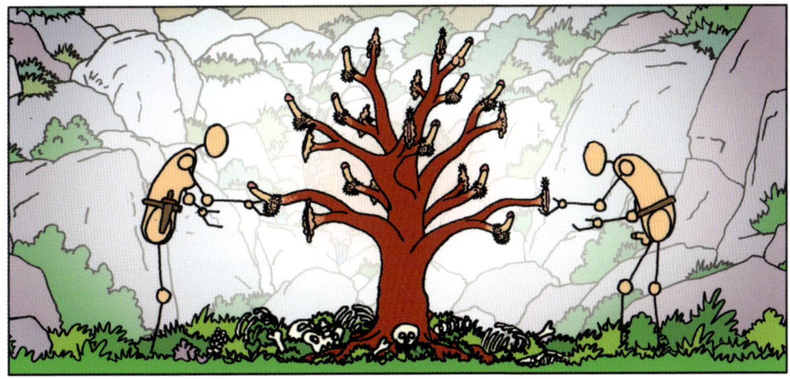

Robert Mapplethorpe

Born in Floral Park, New York, in 1946, Robert Mapplethorpe grew up in a middle class family in Long Island. He attended the Pratt Institute in Brooklyn, where he gained a Bachelor of Fine Arts degree. After graduating, he developed an interest in photography, initially through taking Polaroid photos of himself. In the mid-1970s he acquired more sophisticated photographic equipment and started shooting his friends and acquaintances, moving onto nudes, formal portraits and still-lifes of flowers in the 1980s.

The Perfect Moment exhibition toured the US in 1989 and caused national controversy as the photographs from Mapplethorpe's *X Portfolio* contained images of homoerotic and sado-masochistic acts – images that caused the Corcoran Gallery of Art in Washington, DC, to cancel the exhibition amid concerns over potential loss of future funding. The exhibition later went ahead at another venue with record attendance. Mapplethorpe died of complications from AIDS in Boston, in March 1989.

www.mapplethorpe.org

As part of the infamous *X Portfolio*, this image sat alongside other photographs that all featured images of sado-masochistic sex acts. Fisting, bondage and an explicit self-portrait of Mapplethorpe with a bull-whip inserted in his anus were presented to the viewer. Far from attempting to invite us to the party, these images serve to point out that we cannot get closer to the participants or their activities – the overall aim is to provide a sense of distance – 'look but don't touch'. Indeed, post-AIDS, the freedom of sexual expression typified by Mapplethorpe's work has subsided amongst gay artists.

Sado-masochistic practices are not the preserve of any one particular subculture, and this was something that Mapplethorpe was acutely aware of. Perhaps that is why they provoke a strong reaction – the personal has become public in an overt way. The men in these images are not models – they are private citizens, engaged in a private moment which they have chosen to share with the world at large, offering a critique of a society which hitherto forced everyone to hide their sex lives behind the veil of the illicit.

Mapplethorpe remains culturally significant today in part because of the furore around censorship that arose out of a notorious lawsuit concerning the display of his work. In the early 1990s a court case was brought on charges of obscenity against the director of the Cincinnati Contemporary Arts Center and the centre itself, which had displayed 175 works by Mapplethorpe during a travelling exhibition. Seven images were alleged to be obscene. The Court handed down the decision that Mapplethorpe's images are in fact art, and therefore cannot be categorized as obscene. It was the first time in US history that an arts venue had been prosecuted for displaying an exhibition – the prosecution caused outrage because it contravened the US's First Amendment right to freedom of speech, but it also served to illustrate that some people feel threatened by gay male sexuality.

Jim and Tom, Sausalito
1977
Gelatin silver print
52cm x 127cm
© Robert Mapplethorpe Foundation. Used by permission.

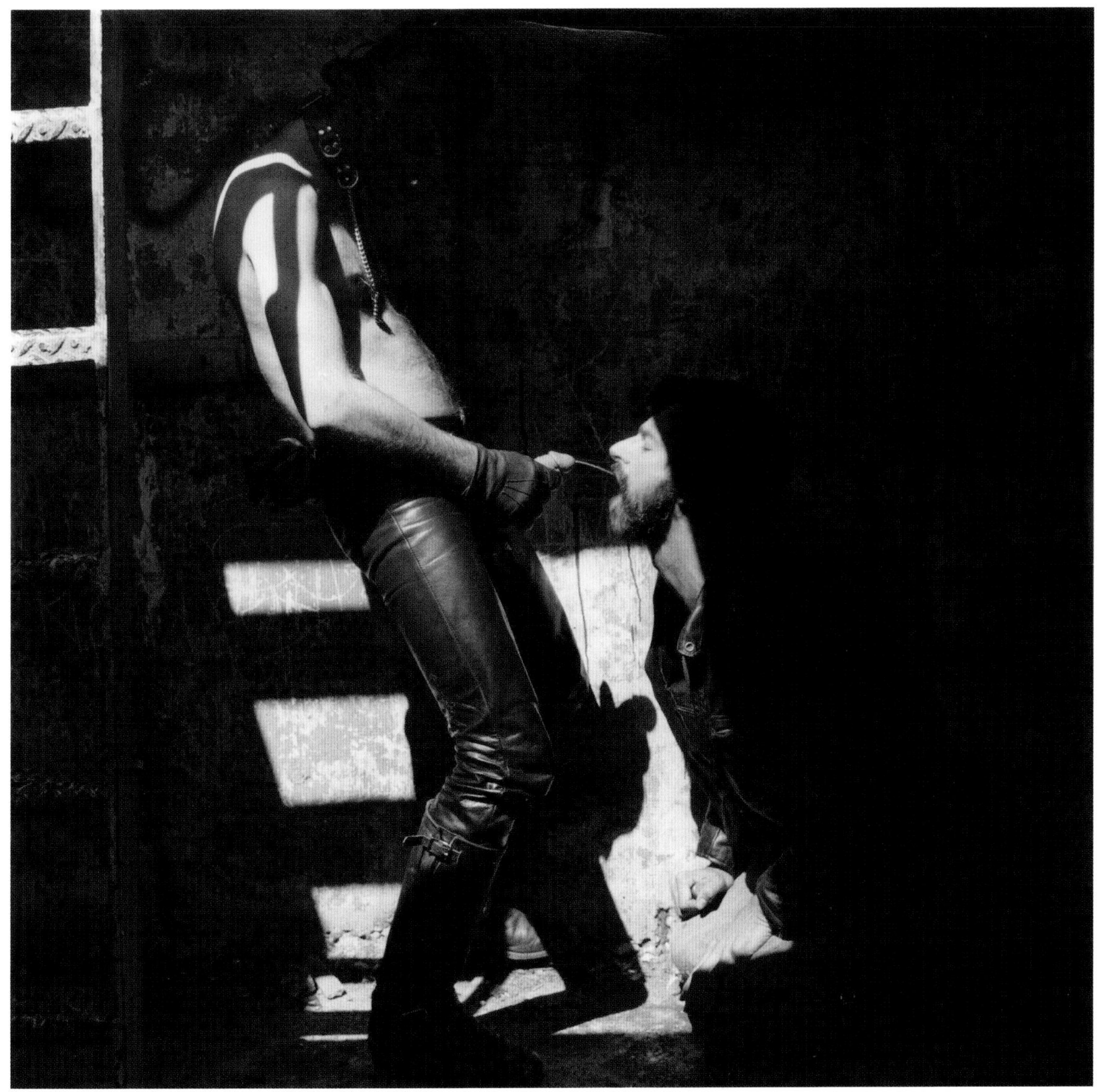

Catherine Opie

Catherine Opie specializes in exploring the community via her documentary photography. She has explored many groups within society, ranging from the LGBT community, through surfers to high school football teams. Opie's work caused controversy in the early 1990s when she created iconic self-portrait works depicting images of cutting and self-mutilation, designed to critique what she saw as the normalization of the queer subculture. Latterly, Opie has become interested in how our identities are shaped by architecture, and in her most recent works she has shifted away from portraiture towards landscape photography and begun examining the positioning of communities in relation to culture.

Born in Sandusky, Ohio in 1961, Opie holds degrees from the San Francisco Art Institute and CalArts. She currently lives and works in Los Angeles. Her work is in the collections of the Museum of Contemporary Art, Los Angeles, and the Museum of Modern Art, New York. She has taught at Yale University and is currently a Professor of Fine Art at the University of California.

Blue sky, warm days and a cool pool – at first glance this photograph draws the viewer into an idyllic scene, one that can only be the refuge of the very wealthy. However on closer inspection we see that the expectant parents are both women, challenging the idea of the nuclear family set-up. One woman seems to be cradling the other in an intimate gesture of protection, staring out at the camera in an unconcerned and indifferent manner, as she floats with her partner in the safety of their private world.

The affluent lifestyle adopted by this family echoes the notion that the couple has reached the pinnacle of an alternative American dream and are untouchable, drifting in their personal realm.

Miggi & Ilene, Los Angeles, California
1995
Chromogenic print
101.6cm x 127cm
Edition of 5
© Catherine Opie, Courtesy Stephen Friedman Gallery,
Regen Projects, Los Angeles, and Gladstone Gallery

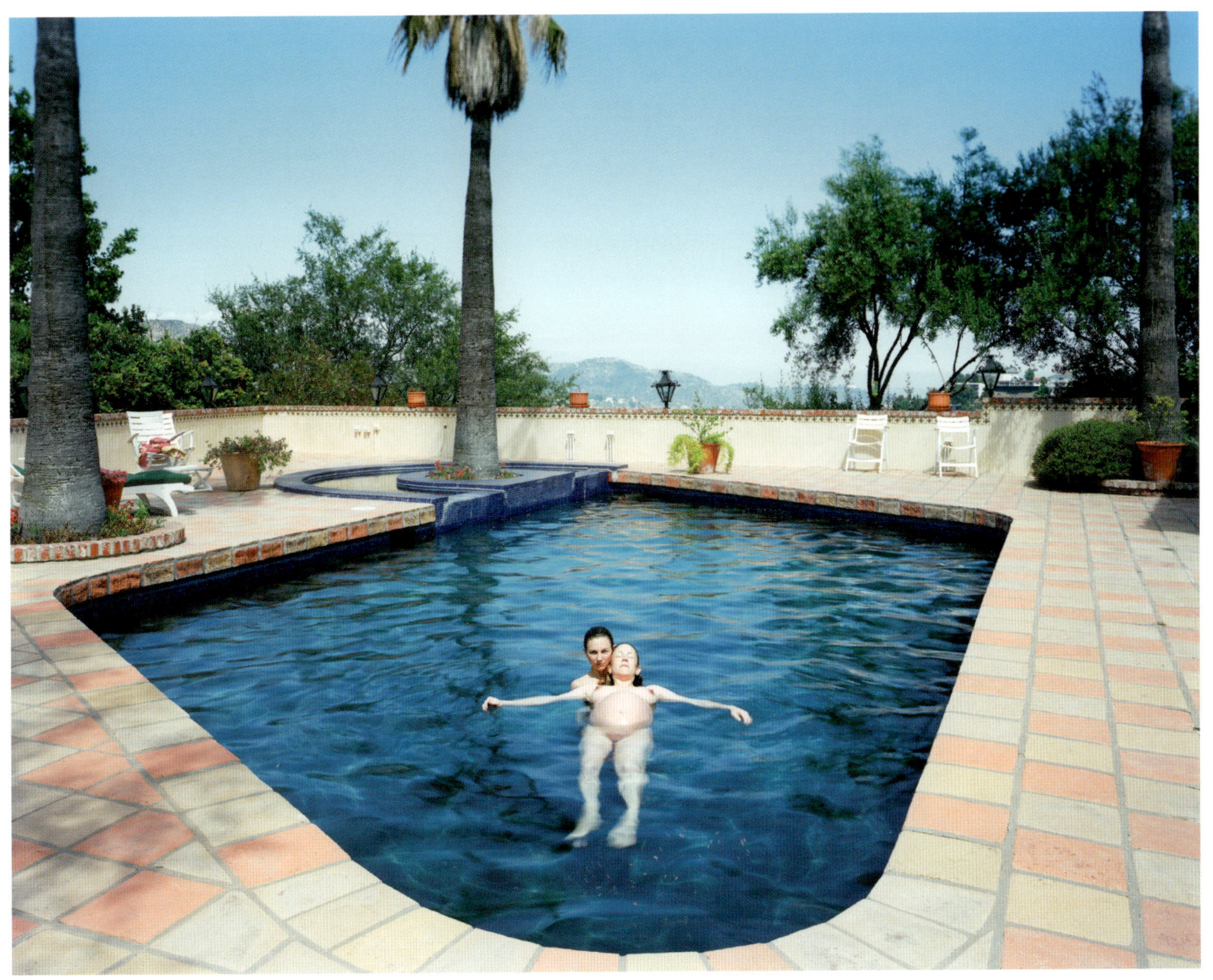

Grayson **Perry**

Grayson Perry is best known for his elaborate ceramic vases, which at a distance seem classically decorative but on closer inspection are covered with narratives and commentaries dealing with aesthetic, cultural, social and political subjects. Winner of the 2003 Turner Prize – which he accepted wearing a purple satin party frock – Perry is also Britain's second most famous transvestite.

Born in Chelmsford, Essex in 1960, Perry studied sculpture at Portsmouth Polytechnic and has worked in a variety of media, including embroidery, film, photography, tapestry, etching and cast metal.

Major solo shows include *Guerrilla Tactics* at the Stedlijk Museum Amsterdam and *The Charms of Lincolnshire* at The Collection, Lincoln and at the Victoria Miro Gallery in London. At present his selection for the Arts Council Collection, *Unpopular Culture*, is touring the UK.

Perry often appears on TV, radio and in the newspapers, commenting on cultural issues, and had a weekly arts column in *The Times* for two years. He lives and works in London.

'There is a lot of ritual around cross-dressing. Approaching the dressing table is akin to approaching an altar of some private religion. Preparations are made in a distinct order. Shaving and perfuming the body, painting the face and nails, putting on the clothes, slipping on the shoes, picking up the handbag, all rites of passage into another world. We are shamans seeking to contact an inner part of ourselves through a ceremony of lipstick, stockings and lace. The transvestite's relationship with the mirror is intimate and charged. It is easy to only see the changes we make to our appearance, focus only on the cosmetics and the dress. But the mirror can be cruel and show us that the paint and finery can only do so much and what stares back at us falls short of a fantasy of femininity. I sometimes find a shadow of tragedy but also a strange nobility in the faces of men who have faced a difficult to deal with part of themselves in the mirror. Coming to terms with a compulsion that causes a man to put himself up for easy mockery and sometimes disgust, leaves a mark beneath the make up.

I have always loved the icons of Orthodox Christianity, the fact that the very artwork itself is venerated and kissed. This ritual of imbuing an object with sacred power is familiar to the fetishist. Every transvestite has favourite moments with magical articles in the transformative process, the application of mascara, zipping up a frock or donning a wig. At their bedroom altars, with the sacraments of femininity, transvestites commune with a mislaid part of their own spirit.'

Transvestite looking in mirror (unfinished)
2009
Ceramic
70cm x 40cm
© Grayson Perry

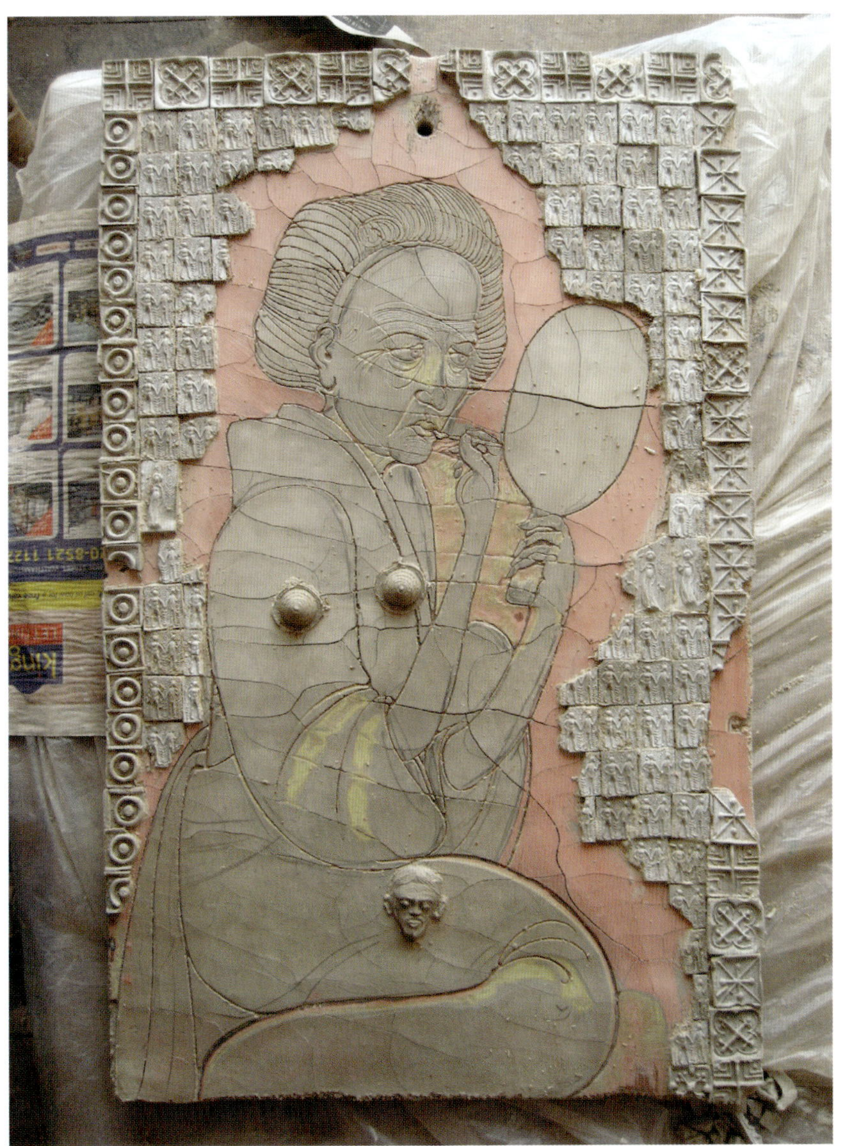

Pierre et Gilles

Pierre et Gilles are French artists who have been collaborating since 1976. As partners they are noted for their highly stylized, sexy, camp photographs, building their own sets and costumes and retouching the images to transport the final art works out of the realms of the real world.

Pierre Commoy, the photographer, was born in the small town of La Roche-sur-Yon in 1949 and studied art in Geneva. Gilles Blanchard was born in Le Havre in 1953 and graduated from the City's École des Beaux-Arts. His early career in advertising laid the ground work for the plasticized glossy look typical of Pierre et Gilles photographs – Blanchard retouches the art works by painting directly onto the prints.

In effect, Pierre et Gilles are perfecting perfection, as unattractive people never feature in their work.

In 2008 they were awarded the CULTURESFRANCE/Créateurs sans frontières Trophy, in recognition of their global success. They live together and work in Paris.

Pierre et Gilles form a couple, an entity whose work is inseparable from their life. They create portraits of stars and unknown people in unique hand painted photographs. They do not use digital software to manipulate the image.

After an initial sketch of the idea they produce a set for the photo shoot in the studio, often using carefully selected materials and accessories that they have collected from world wide travel. Together with careful lighting this animates and magnifies the subject. Finally they conceive a specific frame that is an integral part of the work. Everything is considered in order to achieve an aesthetic perfection.

Two feet on the ground depicts a rent boy or prostitute in Bangkok. There are bars in Bangkok where men parade on stage or around the room with a number on their hip. Clients can ask for the model by number and then move to a nearby room for sex.

This image does not pass any judgement on one of the oldest professions. It depicts a handsome young man posing in front of an opulent background of Thai objects and designs.

A 'curtain' of paint has been applied over the scene giving it the titillation of a peep show. The opening could even be read as a phallic shape. The model has the number 13 and is objectified as beautiful, touching himself as he avoids our gaze.

Two feet on the ground
1999
Unique hand-painted photograph
154.8cm x 124cm
© Pierre et Gilles, Courtesy Galerie Jérôme de Noirmont, Paris

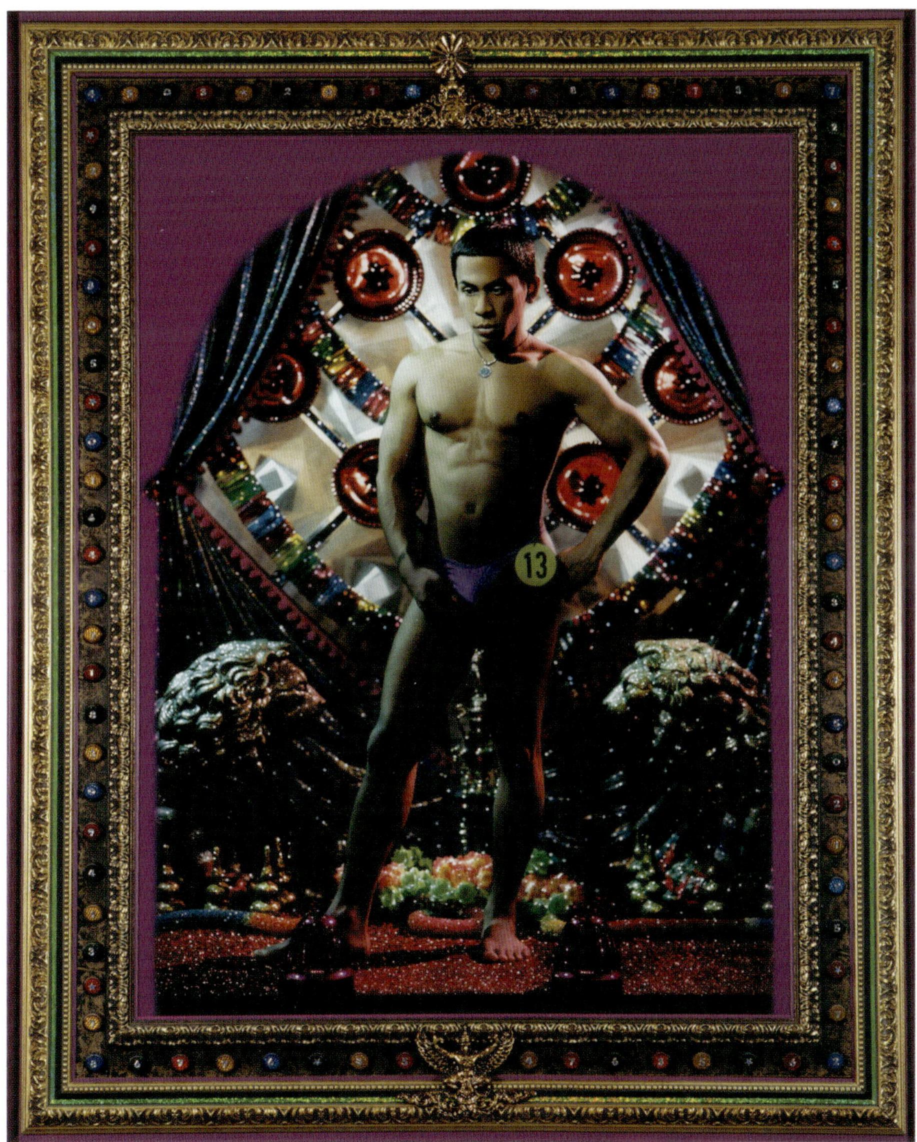

Jack Pierson

Jack Pierson is an American photographer. His body of work includes photographs, collages, word sculptures, installations, drawings and artists' books. He is noted for his celebrated *Self Portrait* series of photographs, looking through the eyes of the desiring viewer at the arc of a man's life span.

Born in 1960 in Plymouth, Massachusetts, he studied at the Massachusetts College of Art and Design, Boston. Pierson's work is held in the collections of the Whitney Museum of American Art, the Guggenheim Museum, the Metropolitan Museum of Art, New York, and the Museum of Contemporary Art, Los Angeles. He has been a Visiting Artist at Yale University, the Museum of Fine Arts in Boston, CalArts in California and MoCA Miami. He lives and works in New York and Southern California.

SELF PORTRAIT #27 is the most youthful image in this exhibition. We are invited to empathize with Pierson's memories of his youth and sexual awakening and recall our own adolescence experiences. Puberty can be a difficult, sometimes lonely time in one's life; however for a young man coming to terms with his homosexuality it can be isolating in the extreme.

It is notable that none of the images in the *Self Portrait* series is in fact a self-portrait of Pierson – instead he establishes a myth of the self, presenting images of others in the manner of his own portrait, claiming their appearance to represent his own identity.

Shot in the studio, this posed image is not glazed, in a deliberate move away from the slickness of glossy photography. The omission is intended to emphasize that it is a fine art print, as opposed to a piece of ephemera.

SELF PORTRAIT #27
2005
Pigment print
135.9cm x 109.2cm
Edition of 7
© Jack Pierson, Courtesy Cheim & Read, New York

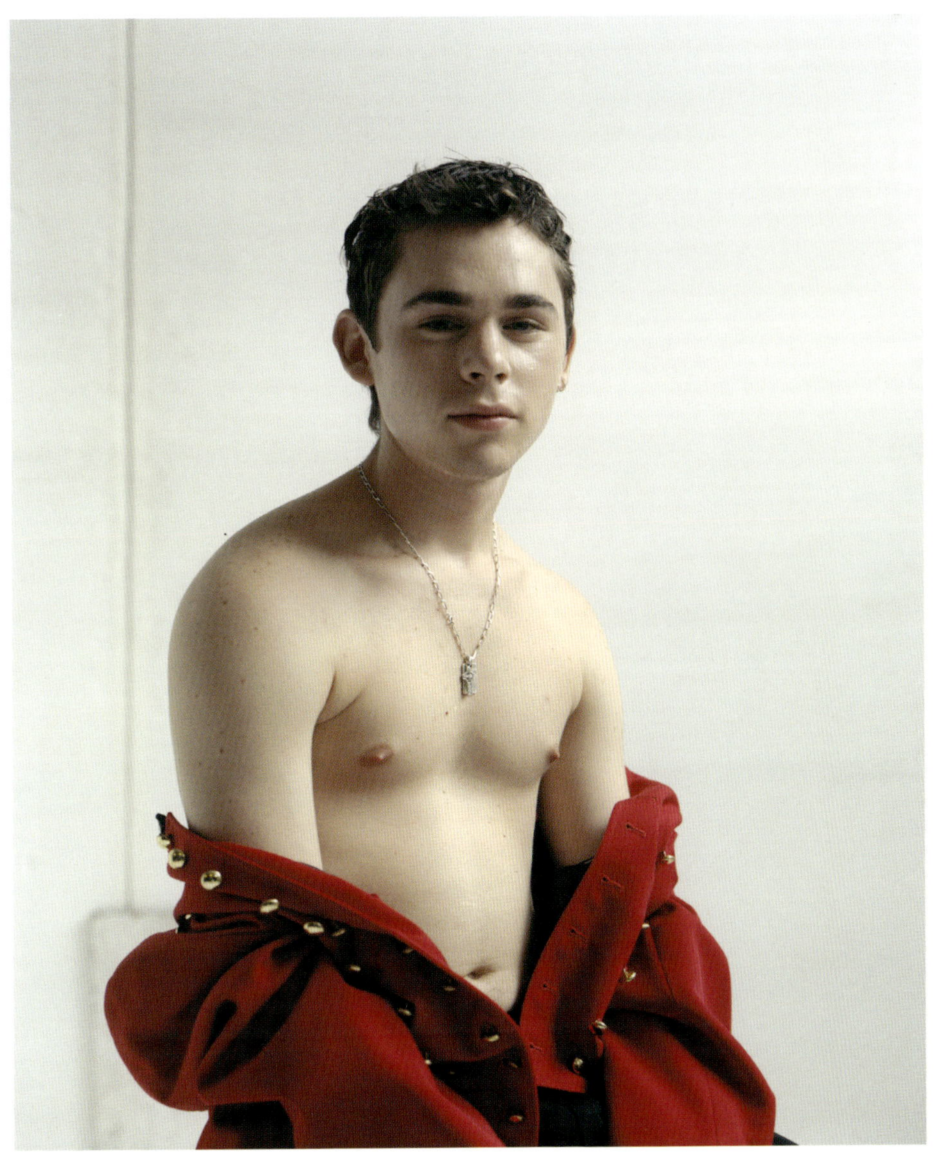

Lizzie **Rowe**

Best known for her autobiographical interiors, still-lifes and self-portraits, Lizzie Rowe continues to draw inspiration from her own experiences and the world of domestic feminine minutiae and is also a sought-after portrait artist. Her work explores costume, perception and the preconceptions society has of a binary notion of gender identity. Her delivery of these explorations emphasizes the reinventions allowed by representative painting.

Born in Portsmouth in 1955 and educated at Reading University's Fine Art Department, Lizzie Rowe worked at Northumbria University until 1998 as a Senior Lecturer in Painting. She has exhibited widely nationally and internationally and her work is held in numerous public collections including the Laden Galerie in Berlin, the Laing Art Gallery and the Theatre Royal in Newcastle, the universities of Durham, Northumbria and Cumbria and Green College, Oxford. Rowe lives and works in Newcastle-upon-Tyne.

www.lizzierowe.co.uk

Lizzie Rowe 'is virtually unique in using her art as an actual means of gender transformation and documentation… she has convincingly embodied this transformation in the genre of immaculately executed figurative painting (which) proves that painting is still a vital creative medium.'
Robert Clark, *The Guardian – Guide supplement*, 2005

In the late 1980s the Newcastle-based 'artist formally known as' Stephen Rowe underwent gender-reassignment to become Lizzie – a personal transformation publicly documented through her paintings and drawings. This self-portrait, the first and, to date, only, nude study from life, marks a watershed in Rowe's personal journey – painted to record her new body after breast augmentation surgery. In a media-obsessed culture where we are bombarded with imagery of 'perfected' femininity a less self-aware painter might have opted for the airbrushed treatment we are taught to aspire to. Here, Rowe aims for an honest 'warts and all' documentary of a transformed mirror image which deliberately highlights the differences in (private) idealized and (public) actual perception of appearance. Painted on rough hessian, as if to remove it further from the slick appearance of the glossy centrefold, the figure gazes out at a sometimes hostile world with a mixture of vulnerability and pride at her new figure. Rowe's yearning and somewhat melancholic statement about aspiring to the unattainable resonates beyond the confines of the gender-dysphoric issues and speaks of a more general twenty-first century malaise. By the same token, the portrait affords a glimpse into an intensely personal goal achieved – honestly and without hyperbole.

Self Portrait with Ribbon and Dress
2002
Oil and wax on hessian
91.4cm x 76.2cm
© Lizzie Rowe

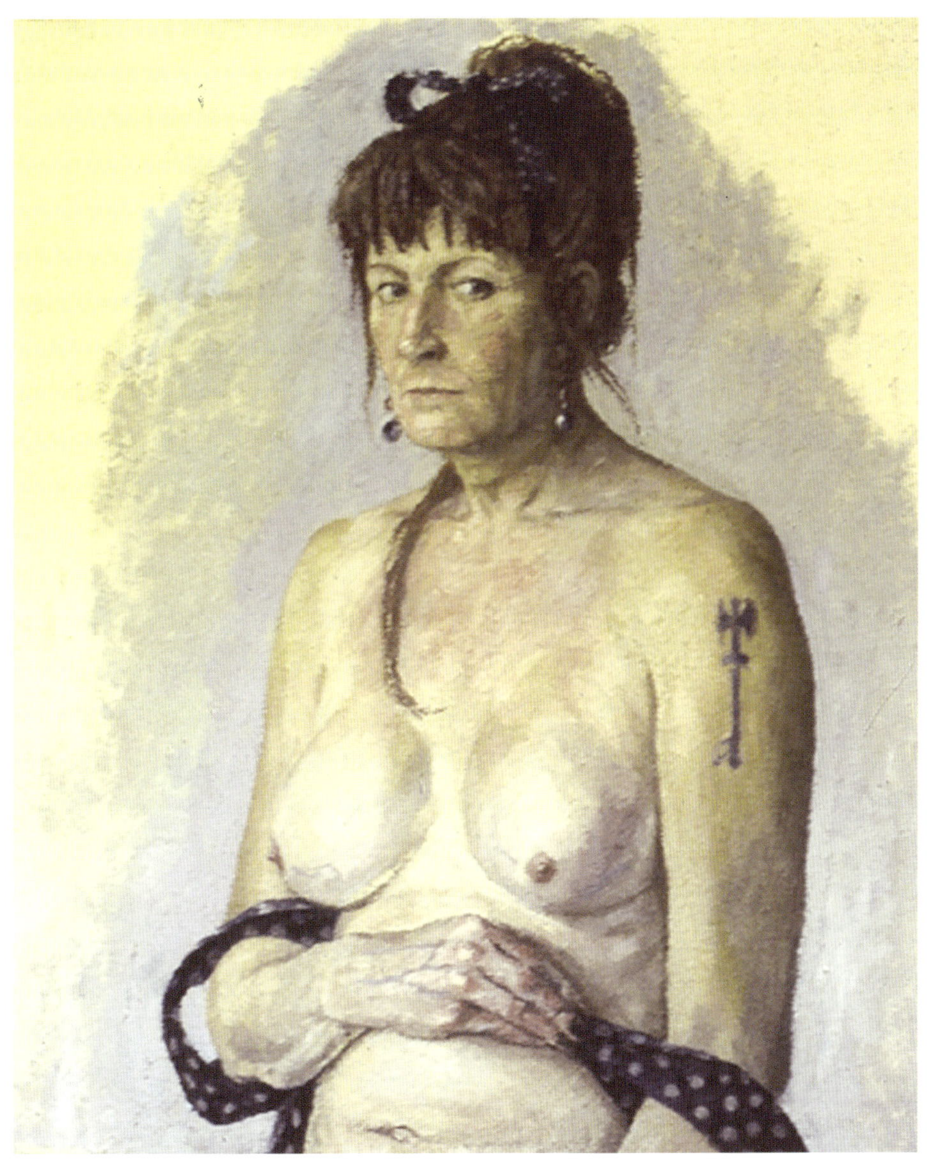

Diane Torr

Diane Torr was born in Ontario, Canada. When she was four, she moved with her family to Aberdeen, Scotland, where she spent her childhood. After graduating from Dartington College of Arts, Devon, Diane returned to North America to develop her career as an interdisciplinary artist, working in the fields of dance, performance, installation, and film. She lived in New York from 1976–2002, and was an integral part of the downtown art scene, presenting at arts venues including Franklin Furnace, The Kitchen, the Mudd Club and Judson Church. A Fellow of the Whitney Museum Independent Study Program, she received her Master of Fine Arts degree from Bard College in Annandale-on-Hudson, New York.

Torr is best known for her performances as a male impersonator, and as an international pioneer of drag king culture.
She has toured and taught Man-for-a-Day workshops in North America, Europe and Asia, and has featured on US and BBC television and in the documentary 'Venus Boyz'.

www.dianetorr.com

'Over the past 27 years my main interrogation, as an artist and activist, has been the narratives of sex and gender. My work has investigated subjects as diverse as feminist go-go dancing and Robert Burns as an icon of Scottish masculinity. From 1996–99 I had a relationship with a woman in Leeds. I was living in New York and travelling to Leeds to visit her on my frequent working trips to Europe. I was astonished to discover homophobia. One day, when we walked down the street holding hands a man shouted "LEZZ-BEE-ANN!" I looked around to see the lesbian. I had no self-consciousness of being a "lesbian". I'm just me. Later, on discovering the high percentage of gay suicide among Yorkshire's teenagers, I was motivated to make an art work that could provoke a dialogue around homophobia, and stereotypes of sex and gender. *IDEAL HOMO* is an installation consisting of a series of photographs, a text and a soundscape that construct a day in the life of two Yorkshire men, Keith and Ricky, who met when working at the Leeds Central Post Office, fell in love and live together. They look like two ordinary blokes. They were, in fact, my lover and myself in drag, although viewers' awareness of that fact depended on how closely they read the catalogue. *IDEAL HOMO* was presented in galleries in Leeds, London, New York and Tokyo. My collaborator, Jane Czyzselska, is currently editor of the lesbian magazine, *DIVA*.'

In 2002 Torr moved to Glasgow, where she is a visiting lecturer at the Glasgow School of Art. She has presented work at the CCA, The Arches and the Tron Theatre. Her book, *Performing Masculinity*, co-authored with Stephen Bottoms, is forthcoming in the autumn of 2009 from the University of Michigan Press.

IDEAL HOMO
1999
Photographic print
61cm x 61cm
Photo: Gordon Rainsford
© Diane Torr

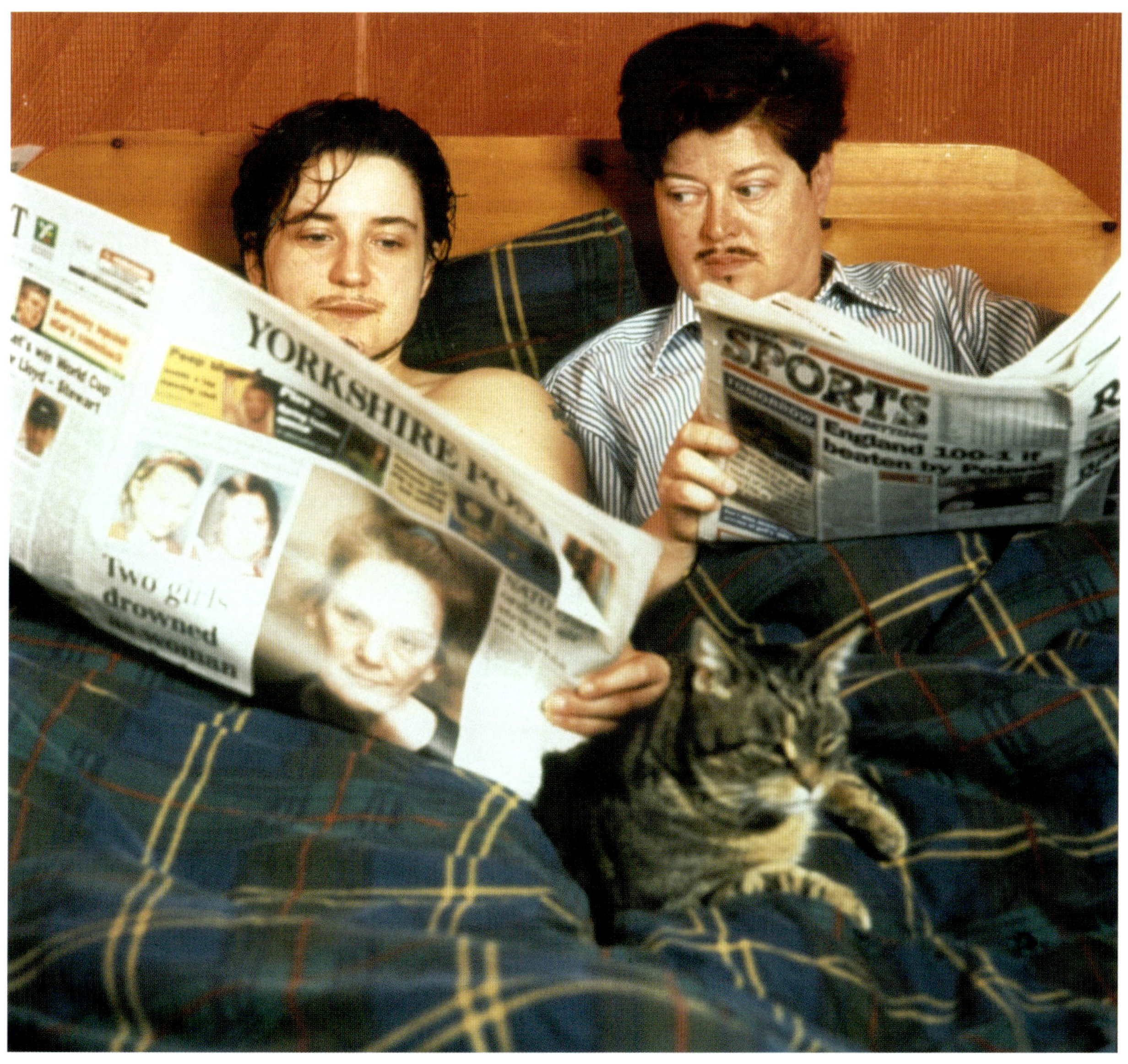
YORKSHIRE POST
Two girls
drowned
SPORTS
England 100-1 if
beaten by Pak

Del LaGrace **Volcano**

Del LaGrace Volcano was born in California in 1957, the Year of the Fire Rooster. Volcano lived the first 37 years of his life as a woman and now lives as an openly transgendered and intersex person. After studying photography at the San Francisco Art Institute in the late 1970s, Volcano gained an MA in Photographic Studies at the University of Derby in 1992. He is considered one of the pioneers of queer photography and has published five books. *Love Bites* (1991) is a photographic monograph of lesbian sexuality. *The Drag King Book* (1999), in collaboration with the academic Judith Halberstam, is the only book to date exploring the lives and performances of drag kings from the USA and Europe, whilst *Sublime Mutations* (2000) is a retrospective of Volcano's photographic work from the 1990s. *Sex Works* (2005) explicitly examines the history of sex in the queer scene and *Femmes of Power* (2008) with the Swedish academic Ulrika Dahl, is the first photographic monograph that celebrates queer and alternative expressions of femininity in the USA and Europe.

www.dellagracevolcano.com

'Volcano's photographs are amongst the most revealing and the most sexual of contemporary images but they always locate his subjects' nakedness in the real of their respective communities.'
Jay Prosser: The Art of Ph/Autography: Del LaGrace Volcano.

'*Herm Torso* was originally entitled "Hermaphrodite Torso" when it was created in 1999 as part of the series *Transgenital Landscapes*. My intention was to problematize the notion of bodily truths and at the same time demonstrate how (physiological) sex is as much of a cultural construct as gender. Although we all know that the relationship between a photograph and the truth is unreliable at best, we still want to believe what our eyes tell us. *Herm Torso* however does not in fact belong to a person who is classified or classifies themselves as a hermaphrodite, but rather to a transsexual man in the process of transition. *Herm Torso* speaks to the truth of corporeal realness, ambiguity and liminality. As Australian art historian Helen McDonald has so aptly stated: "*Herm Torso* proves the gendering function of the gaze to be totally groundless."

It is often assumed that a photographic artist pre-visualizes each image and has absolute control over who, how, where, what and when. I eschew this approach, choosing instead to collaborate and be open to spontaneous occurrence and unknown incident. When the subject of *Herm Torso* arrived at my studio he came pre-inscribed and playful, his chest a board game of noughts and crosses, a fitting metaphor for the impossibility of gender.

My working practice employs what I call a queer feminist methodology – a working ethos committed to making images with speaking subjects rather than taking images from silenced objects. The *process* of creation is as important as the product. There are no victims in my corpus queer, only heroes and stars. Ordinary people living extraordinary lives, but without the safety nets most people take for granted.'

Herm Torso
1999
Giclee print
120cm x 90cm
© Del LaGrace Volcano

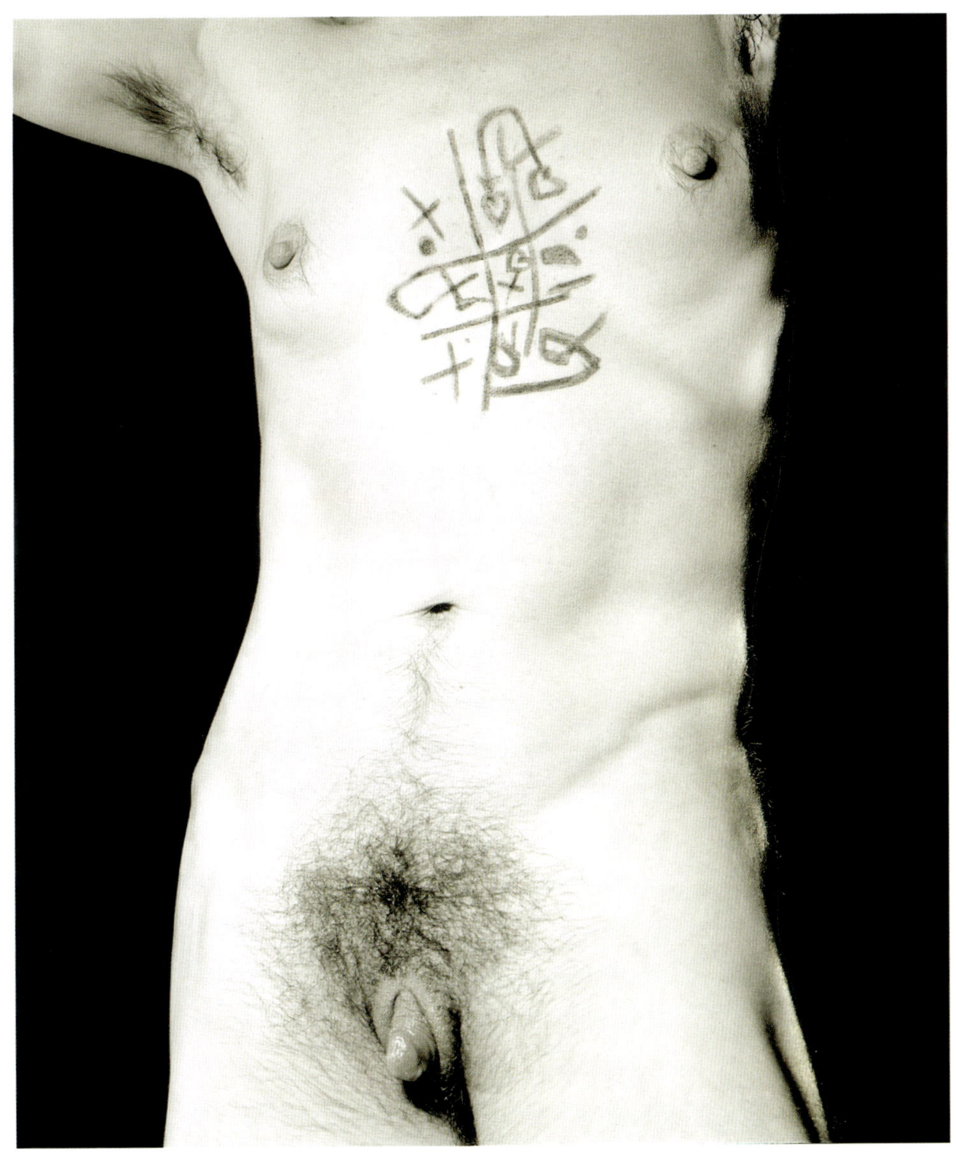

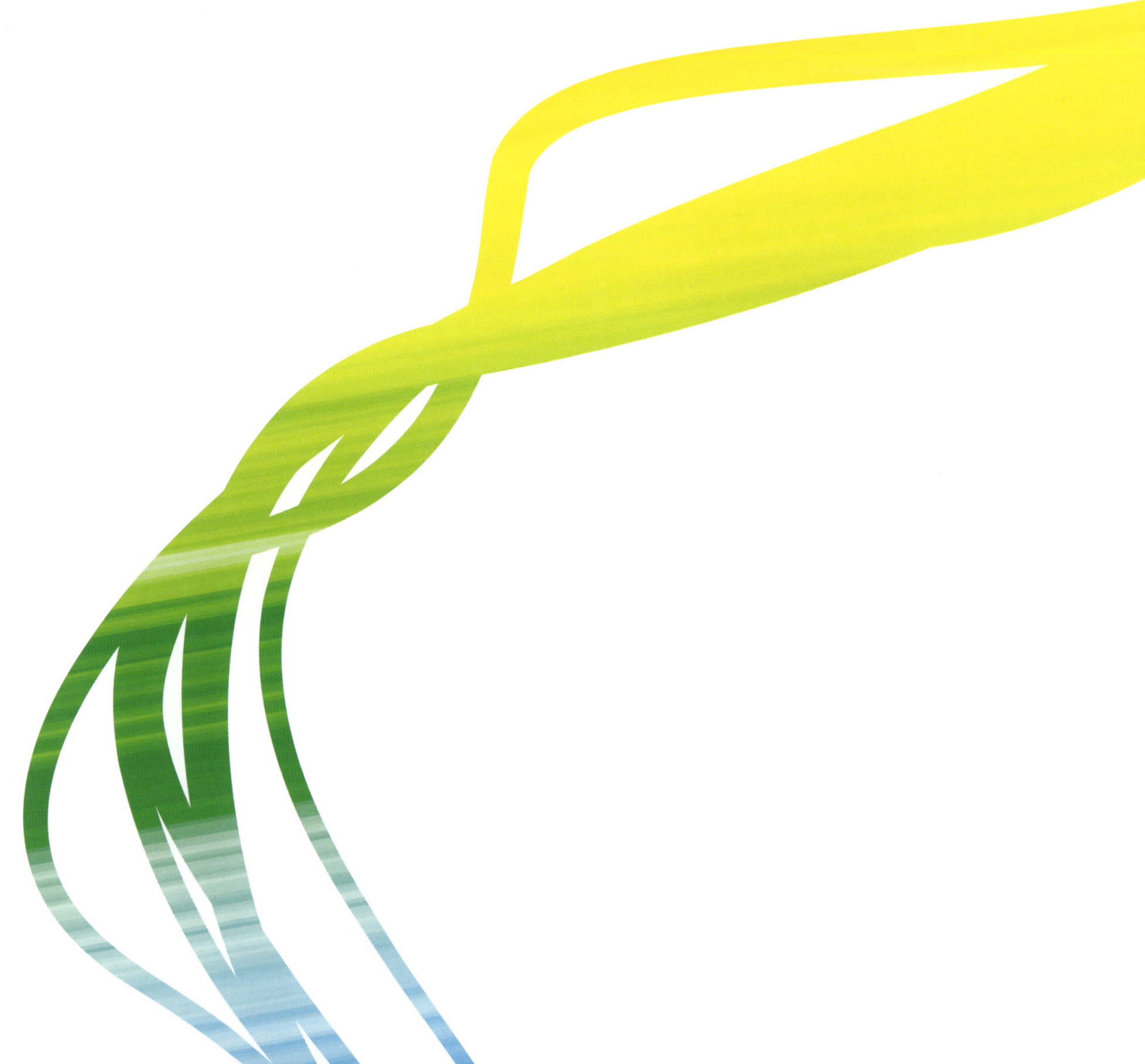

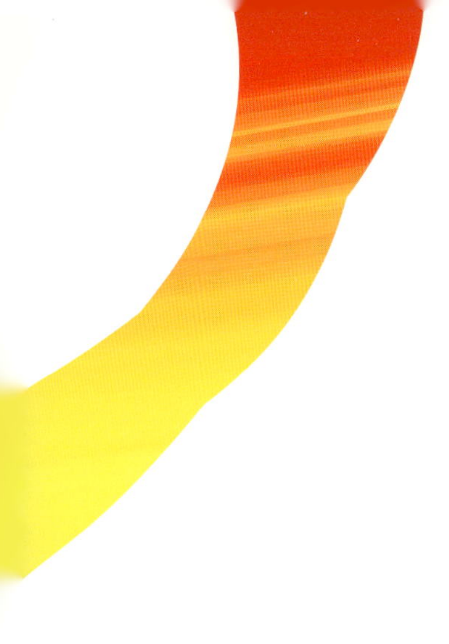

Special thanks to the Culture and Sport Glasgow staff who helped produce the *sh[OUT]* programme and catalogue. Thank you to all the galleries and artists for their help in compiling text and illustrations.

P44 Lizzie Rowe – extract from a review by Robert Clark in *The Guide*, 17 June 2006, © Robert Clark.

P48 Del LaGrace Volcano – extract from the introduction to *Sublime Mutations* published by Konkursbuchverlag, Germany, 2000, © Del LaGrace Volcano.

respect*me*, Scotland's Anti-Bullying Service, was launched in March 2007. It is a Scottish Executive funded service managed by SAMH – the Scottish Association for Mental Health (www.samh.org.uk) – in partnership with LGBT Youth Scotland (www.lgbtyouth.org.uk).

'Dealing with Homophobia and Homophobic Bullying in Scottish Schools: a Toolkit for Teachers' was published in 2008 by LGBT Youth Scotland in association with Learning Teaching Scotland. It can be accessed via the LGBT Youth Scotland website:
www.lgbtyouth.org.uk/schools-and-education-/toolkit.htm.
A copy was sent to every secondary school in Scotland in January 2009.

Addresses

Amnesty International Scotland
Rosebery House
9 Haymarket Terrace
Edinburgh EH12 5EZ
Scotland
Tel (+44) 0844 800 9088
www.amnesty.org.uk

Gallery of Modern Art (GoMA)
Royal Exchange Square
Glasgow G1 3AH
Scotland
Tel (+44) 0141 287 3050
Text phone (+44) 0141 287 3005
Fax (+44) 0141 287 3062
www.glasgowmuseums.com

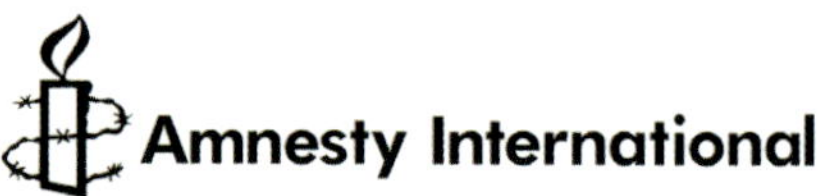
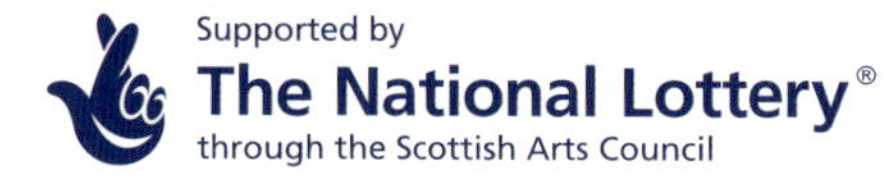

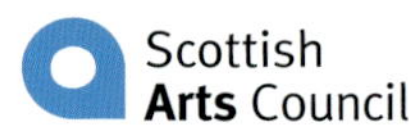

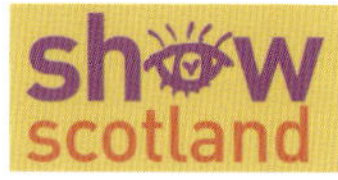
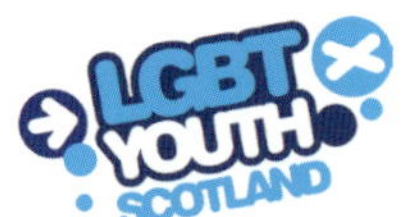
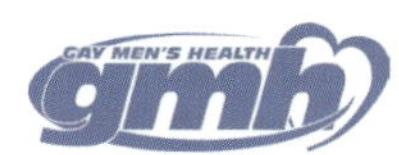
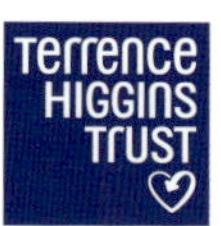
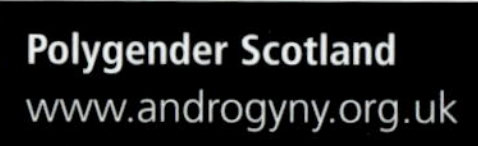

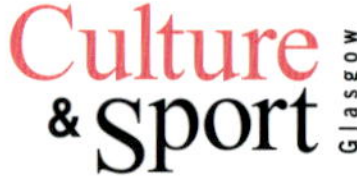
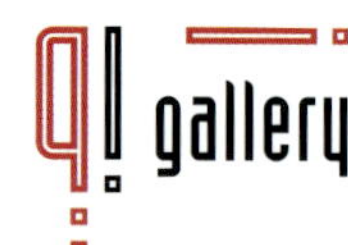
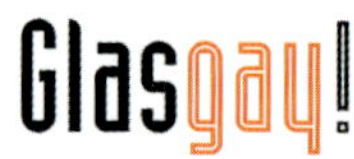
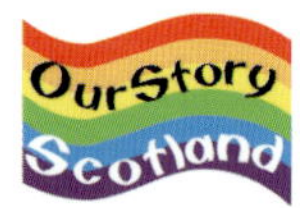
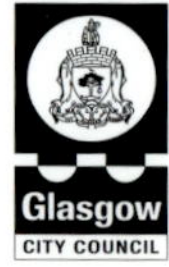